A Funny Thing Happened On ...

THE WAY!

A Funny Thing Happened On...

THE WAY!

Will Pratt

"As soon as they began attacking THE WAY in front of the others, he (Paul) broke with them and took his disciples apart to hold daily discussions in the lecture room of Tyrannus."

(Acts 19:9 - Jerusalem Bible)

WinePress Publishing WP *Mukilteo, WA 98275*

Dedicated to girlfriend Kathleen,

whose own sense of humor—remarkably—has never faltered

since she and I plighted our troth at the altar,

and to son Graeham and daughter Avril, who early learned to

be cheerful under all circumstances.

COVER CARTOON

Just ten days before he died, world famous cartoonist GILES gave the author permission to use his hilarious work, sending his "very best wishes" to The Salvation Army. It appeared the morning after Will Pratt arranged a press call in a Fleet Street pub to show Britain the "new style" Salvation Army uniform. (It had been worn in the States for years!) Gratitude is expressed to the London Daily Express for permission to print.

ACKNOWLEDGEMENTS

I ACKNOWLEDGE MY DEEP INDEBTEDNESS to my many friends who, once it became known I hoped to publish a collection of humorous Salvation Army anecdotes, kindly sent me their recollection of events which—at the time of their happening—had reduced them to near hysterics. Others, known raconteurs of merry tales, to whom I dropped a note wondering if they would want to share some of their gems, were honest enough to reply that when they came to write down their memories, stories which had caused great hilarity when told did not strike them as nearly so funny. I must say, I understand.

It seems from the duplication of tales I have received there are a number of situations which occur remarkably often throughout the Salvation Army world. For example, since the Movement began, preachers and teachers have been losing their dentures right, left and center, and always to the delight of the congregation.

Again, times without number, printers in various parts of the world have omitted the 'e' from the hymn-line, "My God, I am Thine," suggesting that those in the print trade like to brighten (or lighten) their days.

Several well-known personalities seem to have uttered the identical witticism on similar occasions, which brings to mind the comment of philosopher Immanuel Kant: "That is to be expected. Great men are like high church towers; around both there is apt to be a great deal of wind."

So how do I guarantee the authenticity of all the anecdotes and quotes included in this collection? Dear reader, I don't. Since some rely entirely on the memory of the contributor, it would be an impossible task to contact others who could possibly provide corroboration. Instead I rely on the integrity of my contributors.

In the *Faber Book of Anecdotes* (edited by Clifton Fadiman), Leslie Stephen is quoted as saying in his life of Milton that no good story is quite true. "Anecdotes are the thistledown of biography" or, to quote Winston Churchill, "the gleaming toys of history." May no consciences be pricked by these thistledowns as readers play with these toys.

I can well understand Hungarian-born British humorist and writer George Mikes, who decided to undergo psycho-analysis as preparation for writing a book of humor. The analyst began by asking George if he had had a happy childhood.

"I am still having a happy childhood," Mikes responded.

Will Pratt
October, 1996

FOREWORD

Welcome to the world of good humor, good spirit, enrichment. It is Will Pratt, transparent and authentic, bringing to you joy, and helping all of us to a reality of priceless, happy moments on the road of salvation and holiness of heart.

What we laugh at and about is a clear indication of the condition of our hearts and minds. Humor that demeans is no humor at all. Humor that humiliates another, and lessens his concept of what he is, is an assault to his spirit. Christian humor always assumes that it brightens life and encourages the meaning of personal worth.

The humor here is for a Salvationist to laugh at himself. The telling of "Army" stories becomes in the hands of an Army leader—like the erstwhile Public Relations leader for Britain—an exercise in extending the parable-ladened ministry of the Man of Galilee.

The humor here for the non-Salvationist is to look beyond the uniform and the programs of The Salvation Army and meet the people of that Army. Real people. People with the confidence to see our weakness, our strength, our joy, our sorrow, and to understand that we, like all, are human beings. Dedicated human beings. Human beings who tell stories about each other and to each other so that we might become better able to be a part of the paraclete: helpers in The Way. Come laugh with us. Yes, come and feel our humanity with its strengths and weakness. And with its commitment to serve a day that needs some brightening.

The Will Pratt we knew in America was for us a choice leader who never took his own prerogatives as a means to order others. The Will Pratt who compiled the anecdotes and participated in many of them brought joy to the days of his years. We rejoiced with him. We were glad to be in his presence.

He led us into the presence of God with rare good spirit and joy. Welcome!

It is for Mrs. Miller and myself a thrill to be again *with* Will and Kathleen Pratt in a special ministry to our Lord by being allowed to introduce you to this work and this ministry of elation and relation.

"Be glad in the Lord and rejoice"—

"Rejoice, and again I say rejoice, for the Lord is at hand."

I thank my God for every thought of you. And yours. And our inner happiness and our laughter *with* each other.

God bless you, richly.
Andrew Miller
Commissioner (R)

Lawrenceville, Georgia
October 1996

ABOUT THE AUTHOR

WILL PRATT became a Salvation Army officer in 1947, after three years in the British Royal Navy. His parents, two brothers and sister all became officers. His father was the first Salvation Army officer to be killed on duty in England during World War II.

Pratt served for sixteen years in the Salvation Army editorial department in London, England. A twelve-week tour of the Far East, reporting and photographing a campaign by General and Mrs. Wilfred Kitching, was one highlight. Three thirty-minute 16mm film documentaries, the book *Tell Them in the East*, and numerous photographs and reports resulted.

From editorship of *The Musician,* he became Information Services Officer just prior to the Army's hectic centennial celebrations in 1965. For seven years, he was spokesperson for the Army at International Headquarters, liaising with media and broadcasting on BBC. He then became Public Relations Secretary.

Pratt and his wife, Kathleen, were appointed to the USA Western Territory in January 1978, he serving as Chief Secretary. In 1982, he became Territorial Commander and Kathleen, Territorial President of Women's Organizations. They held the same positions in Canada from 1984 and retired from Toronto in 1990.

They have two children and four grandchildren.

William Booth, founder of The Salvation Army, once said "Why should the devil have all the best tunes?" If Will Pratt's book had been written when he was alive, Booth might have added, "And why should the devil have all the best jokes?"

Humor in The Salvation Army is great stuff, and all the merrier because it's a factual account of real happenings. I guess it's not only prayer, preaching and brass bands that keep the Army going, but fun and laughter, too.

Bob Hope
October, 1996

CONTENTS

AN EXPLANATION

THE SPECIAL GRACE OF THE SALVATIONIST?

A GRIZZLED RETIRED SALVATION ARMY OFFICER was being quizzed on his ninetieth birthday by a television reporter. "What are the essential qualifications for a successful Salvation Army officer?" she asked him.

The old boy's eyes twinkled. "A sense of humor and no sense of smell," he answered.

A young Lieutenant, newly commissioned from the training college, might well have answered far more circumspectly with such orthodox and very correct replies as "dedication to God" or "burning compassionate love for one's fellow men." Not so this seasoned campaigner. He took such qualities for granted. Who in his right mind would offer for Salvation Army officership unless dropped on his head when a baby, or called by God and in love with faltering humanity? After all, were not Army officers commissioned to "hard labor for life," to quote the whimsical William Booth, Founder of the Army?

Long experience had taught the ninety-year-old that even the most dedicated and loving had sometimes not been able to endure and had fallen by the wayside. Such are the demands made on officers, and so rugged the conditions in which at times they will be expected to serve, that things will go hard with them unless additionally they have been endowed with a delicious sense of humor and a strong enough stomach to ignore what their olfactory organ was telling them.

For many Salvation Army officers, humor is an expression of determination not to let "them"(whoever "them" may be) get you down. It's a halfway stage between at worst a deadly cynicism or at best the triumph of hope and faith in one's cause and achievement.

The essential joyfulness of the real Salvationist was recognized by the one hundredth Archbishop of Canterbury and Primate of All England, Dr. Michael Ramsey, when he addressed the opening ceremony of the Army's centennial celebrations in 1965. With Her Majesty the Queen taking central place on a platform packed with ambassadors, diplomats, church leaders, politicians, the great and the good, and some 5,000 people crowding the Royal Albert Hall, the Archbishop said in his slow, deliberate, impressive way: "Among the many things I have seen, the one thing I have never seen is a g-l-o-o-m-y Salvationist."

Some of us there held our breath and silently thanked God he had never been to our corps. But Dr. Ramsey was right. The occasional gloom-and-doom merchant is an out-of-character oddity, totally inconsistent with the Army's history and essential spirit. Those somewhat severe navy-blue uniforms may give an impression of unrelieved solemnity to the public (why a light-grey suit such as that worn by our officers in Zimbabwe has not become standard wear is a mystery), but closer acquaintance with any group of Salvationists is a guaranteed introduction to their natural jollity—as I believe this anthology will show.

Religion and gloom are, of course, synonymous in many people's minds. That is well illustrated by the old story of the two Englishmen traveling by train in typical stony silence. Eventually one spoke: "Pardon my asking, but are you a clergyman?" Blushing, the other replied, "No, indeed not. I'm just recovering from influenza."

Even within religious circles, where they should know better if they study their New Testament, the person of humor and wit is sometimes thought of as a lightweight. Conversely, the person of ponderous expression and unrelieved solemnity is regarded with much respect as a deep thinker.

"Make him (the reader) laugh and he will think you a trivial fellow. But bore him in the right way and your reputation is assured," declared W. Somerset Maugham in *The Gentleman in the Parlour*.

Sydney Smith (1771-1845), a British clergyman and author, was a celebrated wit and a favorite in London society after he moved south from Edinburgh. There he had been part of a circle of brilliant politicians and philosophers. His brother Robert was also a clergyman. But Robert attained much higher eminence in the church than did Sydney. With a sigh, Sydney observed: "Robert rose by gravity; I sank by levity."

All too often the cause of Christ has been harmed by the totally false notion that to be sincere you must be deadly serious. But when St. Paul lists what he calls "the fruit of the Spirit" (Galatians 5:22,23)—that is, those characteristics which identify a person in whom God the Holy Spirit lives and reigns—he first mentions love, then follows it immediately with joy. Now no one can claim he was listing these "fruits" in order of importance, but quite clearly love and joy went hand-in-hand in his thinking. One hears a great deal about love, love, love from pulpit and platform, but not nearly so much about joy.

In his book, *The Everlasting Man*, G.K. Chesterton writes: "Joy, which was the small publicity of the pagan, is the gigantic secret of the Christian." He goes on to ponder the qualities of "the tremendous figure which fills the gospels," mentioning Christ's pathos, never concealing his tears nor his anger, as he flung furniture down the front steps of the temple. "Yet," writes Chesterton, "He restrained something. I say it with reverence; there was in that shattering personality a thread that must be called shyness. There was something that he hid from all men when he went up into a mountain to pray. There was something that he covered constantly by abrupt silence or impetuous isolation. There was some one thing that was too great for God to show us when he walked upon our earth; and I have sometimes fancied that it was his mirth."

Fanciful or not, I have no problem in believing the Almighty has a tremendous sense of humor. I have watched our twin grandchildren grow and develop since day two.

They grinned at me the moment they saw me, I swear, though the maternity nurse scorned my naiveté and assured me they had wind. Thankfully, their wind has moderated, but the mirth which the nurse said was not there has developed marvelously.

Now, no one has taught them to grin, to smile coyly, to chuckle and even to laugh quite boisterously, but before they were six-months-old they were expert little clowns. They have needed to be taught many things, but the Great Creator equipped them with a mirth machine before they arrived. And since God gave them this gift of laughter, then he must possess that gift himself. He could not give them what he does not have.

Mrs. Commissioner Flora Larsson asserts that the Creator who made giraffes and kangaroos quite definitely revealed a sense of humor. She adds: "Each time I see those animals I enjoy a joke with him." She explains the Creator's purpose through the poem of F.W. Harvey:

He made the comical ones, in case
the minds of men
should stiffen and become
dull, humorless and glum:
And so forgetful of their Maker be
as to take themselves...
quite seriously.

One of the reasons for the sweeping success of The Salvation Army in its earliest days was the exuberant joy of the Salvationists. They sang their praises to God with gusto. They banged their tambourines, clapped their hands, roared forth their hallelujahs. And the common people heard them gladly. There was an infectious gaiety about their worship.

Army history books tell of the occasion when the celebrated organist of Harrow Public School (where Sir Winston Churchill was a less-than-satisfactory pupil) decided to see for himself what these first Salvationists were up to. He arrived at the meeting rather late and the only available seats were those at the front, near to the brass band—indeed near to the bass drummer. After that good bandsman had thwacked the quivering hide through a couple of songs, the sensitive musician, Dr. Farmer, leaned over and begged him not to hit the drum so hard.

The cockney beamed at him and replied, "Lor' bless yer, sir, since I've been converted, I'm that 'appy I could bust the bloomin' thing."(It is testimony to his conversion that he said "bloomin"!)

Inevitably, thankfully, techniques and skills are vastly advanced today in all realms of the Army's services and worship. But Salvationists treasure their heritage. While they don't *live* in the past, they know they must *live up* to the past. The freedoms, the merriment, the joy are a precious inheritance they must not lose. It is a gift from God himself to a Movement that he raised up to be a commando force. And because time and time again something funny happens on THE WAY, they see that he uses even those situations to his glory. For spirits are cheered, loads lightened, tensions lessened and energies to do God's work redoubled.

As General W. Bramwell Booth (son of the Army's Founders) remarked: "I have sometimes dared to think that humor was one of the special graces of Salvationism."

Will Pratt

CHAPTER 1

WE'LL NEVER LET THE OLD FLAG FALL

THERE IS A TIME EACH YEAR WHEN BULBS peek through the earth. There is another time when leaves fall from the trees. So is there a time each year in the Salvation Army world when its officers tremble, either with apprehension or anticipation. The technical name for this trembling is "farewell-itis."

In May in the United Kingdom, and other months elsewhere around the world according to clime, headquarters brass hats determine whether an officer shall remain in his or her appointment or move elsewhere. Since the farewell may mean transferring from one end of the country to another or even from one country to another, the trembling is understandable. Happily, the vigor with which the brass hats once reshuffled their personnel has somewhat abated. (Unless they enjoy evoking hilarity, non-U.K. readers are advised not to use the term "long stays" when visiting Britain. It will be taken to mean a stiffened bodice or corset.)

Two bolt-from-the-blue appointments in 1949 totally

knocked off course what I had imagined would be my career as a Salvation Army officer. From being a carefree, independent commanding officer in charge of my lovable flock at Sheerness Corps, mixing with fellow ministers and able to roam at will as we sought to bring about the salvation of the Isle of Sheppey, I was to become a back-room boy at International Headquarters in the Editorial Department.

I trudged gloomily behind my new boss, Major Sidney Williams, editor of *The Musician*, to which I had been appointed, as he introduced me to editors and staff in their lairs bearing the name of their periodical. He did his best to cheer me. At a door marked "Men Only" he commented, "We don't have an editor for that." I began to feel more at home. At least he was human.

My apprehension had to do with knowing I was to take over the duties of popular Salvation Army music composer, choral conductor and trainer, Brindley Boon, who was entering the Army's officer-training college. On my first visit to the International Music Editorial Department, where cub reporters were sent to gather copy, I confessed my fears to Lt.-Colonel Albert Jakeway. That blunt, square-jawed, distinguished musician lied wonderfully. "You're as good as him, any day," he said.

I began to feel that maybe I could learn to do the job. Then came bolt-from-the-blue number two. "Colonel Norman Duggins wants to see you," Sid Williams told me. No, he didn't know why. I felt strange forebodings all over again. The Colonel was Chief Secretary to the Chief of the Staff, the Army's second-in-command, and regarded as very much "the power behind the throne." What had I done wrong?

Like a surgeon feeling for the right place to insert the scalpel, he inquired how I was settling in to International Headquarters. I was about to tell him when he dropped his bombshell. "The Chief of the Staff has appointed you to the International Staff Band in addition to your editorial duties." I felt myself go pale as I thought, "They can't have heard my cornet playing." But Colonel Duggins' next words made it clear they weren't interested in my cornet playing. "The Chief has appointed you as Flag Officer," he said with the beatific look of a man who expected me to go down on my knees with gratitude.

I was too shell-shocked to wonder why the Chief of the Staff, second-in-command of the entire Salvation Army world, even then at work in eighty-five countries, should ever bother himself appointing anybody to carry the Staff Band flag. But the Colonel, who also served as executive officer for the band, was determined to make me realize that heaven itself could bestow no greater honor.

I left his office in a daze. The very thought of marching at the head of that band of all bands—those ultra efficient, highly critical men—paralyzed me. I had never carried a flag in my life. There had always been taller, more brawny, more worthy fellows than I.

As with the editorial job, my worries about the Flag Officer role were intensified because of my predecessor. I was to succeed Major Fred Biggs, a naturalized Britisher whose homeland was Germany. He had transferred to Britain after the war with Germany, where he had endured much suffering for his faith under the Nazis.

Now Fred embodied all that was best in the Prussian military regime. Of upright bearing—arm-swinging, heel-clicking—he was an ideal flag-wagger. What chance did I stand, a former war-time civilian in sailor's clothing, a conscripted Royal Navy man! The navy's marching skills had been well summed up by that Admiral of the Fleet who commenced a march-past at Portsmouth by announcing, "Royal Marines will march past in columns of fours; Royal Navy will follow in a horrible big heap."

Fred handed over to me all the gear: large white leather gloves, white leather strap with holster, double white cord with knotted tassels to tie round the beautiful chromium ISB crest which I would screw onto the top of the flag. He explained that because the band was always in transit to appointments—bus, train, sea or air—the two flagpoles which joined together were kept in a long leatherette case. As for the actual flag—that is the bunting—on which were emblazoned the names of all the countries in which the band had campaigned, that was to be carefully folded after each engagement and placed at the bottom of the skip—a wicker basket in which the bandsmen's red, lion-tamer stripe uniforms were transported.

(In due time I saw that even if my flag had to be carefully folded, the red tunics certainly were not, but flung hurriedly by their wearers into the skip after a perspiringly hot two and a half-hour music festival and the lid clamped down with a locked steel bar. The linkage with the lion-tamer image seemed all the stronger.)

I did my best to thank Fred. He parted with these treasures sorrowfully. I took them home and, aided by my dutiful but wondering wife, sought to restore them to pristine glory. At least the flag must look great, no matter how the new Flag Officer carried it.

My first weekend with the band was at Sholing, Southampton. The Saturday night festival was held in a large church in Southampton, there being no hall in Sholing adequate to contain the expected congregation. I sat with the two percussionists and tried to look like a musician with no part to play, while trying not to think about the next morning when I would carry the flag for the first time along the streets of Sholing to the open-air meeting.

Following early Sunday morning prayers, there was a hustling and bustling as the Staff Bandsmen found and opened their instrument cases and prepared to form up for the march. I assembled my twin flagpoles, screwed on the chromium top, tied on the gleaming-white cord and tassels, so expertly laundered by my beloved, and looked for the skip to unearth the flag.

"Anybody seen the skip?" I shouted with some sense of panic. "It's still at the church in Southampton for this afternoon's festival," someone shouted back. No one had thought to tell the raw, rookie Flag Officer that I should have removed my flag the night before.

Carrying my flagpole, starkly bare but for the tasseled chromium crest, and wearing my brilliant white gauntlet gloves and strap, I made my way apprehensively to the Staff Bandmaster, the inscrutable Major Bernard Adams. Even his few close friends never took liberties with Bernard Adams. Well-educated, brilliant cornet soloist, masterful conductor, he had the kind of wit which usually left him the winner in any repartee.

It was a mark of my innocence that I chose to approach the awesome Staff Bandmaster about the absent flag. In all the corps bands in which I had played, the bandmaster was solely in charge and handled any problems. Not this one.

"P-p-please Bandmaster," I began, stuttering a little as I realized how ridiculous it was that my first conversation with this great one was to tell him that his new Flag Officer had just lost his flag, "the skip with the flag in it is still in the Southampton church." Faltering as my words dried up, I gestured toward my naked flag pole.

His face remained impassive. "That's bad luck," he commented. "Why don't you tie a text on the top of it?"

Leaving me speechless, he made his dignified way through the hall exit to take up his position at the head of the march.

A cold fury suddenly possessed me. I thrust the flagpoles back in their case and hurried the tassels and flag top away. Then without a request to anyone, I seized the Sholing Band flag from its socket on the hall platform and scurried outside to join the waiting bandsmen.

My worst fears were being confirmed already. I knew I was not cut out to be the Flag Officer of the international Salvation Army's premier band. Here, on the very first occasion when I was supposed to be carrying the greatly esteemed flag of a band that had been famous since its inception in 1891, I was marching along with the Sholing Band flag. But it wasn't my fault, I argued to myself. I hadn't wanted this so-called honor. Besides, they weren't being very nice to me.

But abruptly my soliloquizing ended. In this quiet Sunday morning street I suddenly realized I could hear no marching

5

feet. What had happened? Where were they? Still marching, I half-turned to see. THEY WERE AT LEAST FIFTY YARDS BEHIND ME. With my thoughts in angry turmoil, I had been tramping on with lengthened stride, eager to get this first calamity behind me and give the Sholing man his flag back. And they had let me!

I halted and waited the eternity until the band, behind the now smiling Bandmaster Adams and Executive Officer Colonel Norman Duggins, had caught up with me. Executive Officer? Executioner Officer indeed, I growled to myself!

Four weeks later I had to face my second weekend campaign with the I.S.B. We were to visit Kettering, the heartland of brass banding in Britain. The likelihood of so many expert performers and keen music critics being in the audiences prompted even the imperturbable Bandmaster Adams to remark during the eve-of-departure rehearsal: "We'd better be on our toes this weekend."

In the event, I was almost on my knees.

Still smarting from the humiliation of my experience at Sholing, I resolved that no part of that famous flag would be out of my sight at any time during the weekend. Even if I did not want to be made a Flag Officer, I wanted still less to be made a fool of again. This weekend I would show them.

Sunday morning came. Trembling a little with anticipation I assembled my flag—all of it. The two halves of the pole interlocked nicely. I screwed in the beautiful chromium-plated crest atop the pole and neatly tied the gleaming-white long tassel cord to it. Wearing my long, white leather gauntlet gloves, I hoisted my flag into the shining chromium socket held by my equally gleaming white leather strap. The drummer tapped the beat, and away I strode at the head of the Army's premier band.

Now on two or three occasions I had admired my predecessor, the good Fred Biggs, marching ahead of the I.S.B. When the column was to turn left or right at a street corner, Fred would march on to the center of the road, then dramatically dip his flag and swing it toward the new direction to be taken. With a deft swirl, he would then bring it back to the upright position and march forward to lead the band along the new route. I decided that honor dictated I should try my hand at this.

It was a moment of foolish ambition. I had actually rehearsed the maneuver in the hallowed Assembly Hall of the International Training College, scene of many solemn occasions and resting place of the flags of each session of officer-cadets trained there. When no one was looking, I had taken the current session's flag and marched up and down the aisles practicing the dipping of the banner. Apart from its digging in the area of my appendix, I thought I handled it reasonably well.

With hindsight, I know I should have practiced with the Staff Band flag for, without my knowing it, the top of the flagpole was gradually being worn by the repeated screwing-on and withdrawal of the crest.

The first corner of the Kettering Street was now upon me. I dipped the flag down. Forcefully, I swung it to the left. There was a flash of chrome as my gleaming I.S.B. crest shot like an arrow toward the ear of Eddie Scotton, the bass trombonist at the end of the front-line trombonists. (Had he been the servant of the high priest in the New Testament, he could not have looked more startled!)

Worse was to follow. As I smartly raised the pole to the upright position, the beautifully woven flag, no longer held by the crest but only by the chromium rings, came rattling down the pole to smother me completely, leaving me unable to see. The famous Staff Band's sweet Sunday morning hymn-tune resolved itself into the sounds of a solitary bass and second baritone um-pahing as the other bandsmen stopped playing and choked with laughter.

Above the pandemonium came the Cockney voice of the band's secretary, Senior-Captain Frank Lyndon, in the solo cornet section: "Crikey, boys," he yelled, "he's dedicating himself!"

One would have thought that two successive weekends of misadventure would have been too much for the stately

I.S.B's image. Perhaps curiosity to see what possible further antics I could achieve with their precious emblem prompted the authorities not to replace me immediately with a more worthy fellow. But my term as flag wagger continued for a further twelve months, and even then did not end because of misdemeanor. After an operation for appendicitis (had I dug the flagpole in too hard?) it was mercifully agreed that I should no longer lift up the banner. Instead, I joined the 2nd cornet section—regardless of my skills.

The final twelve months included heading the march through the gates of Buckingham Palace for a royal command performance in the forecourt to mark the band's 60th anniversary. I prayed no misadventure would befall me on this most prestigious of occasions.

Actually I was not feeling well. Although I did not know it, not only I but my appendix was grumbling. As the band played to His Majesty, I began to feel sick. *The Musician* editor, my boss Sid Williams, was standing beside me. I thrust the flag into his hands without explanation and hastily disappeared round a corner of the famous palace.

I think I can claim to be the only Salvation Army officer who has puked down a royal drain.

CHAPTER 2

BLOOD AND FIRE TRAINING

T HE OBJECTIVE OF THE SALVATION ARMY'S officer training colleges (covering more than one hundred countries where the Army is at work) has been concisely defined for its training staff. They are to produce "Blood and Fire officers." As long ago as 1884, Catherine Booth, co-founder with husband William, described in six precise points the method of training the Movement's future officers:

1. We begin with the heart. 2. We try to train the head. 3. We teach them how to appeal to the consciences of the people. 4. We teach them how to inspire hope in the most hopeless. 5. We try to show them how to exhibit the Savior as a full, sufficient sacrifice for sin. 6. We teach them how to utilize the trophies they may be permitted to win.

Dr. William Barclay, brilliant world-renowned New Testament scholar, wrote in 1960: "The notable thing about this document is that, although it is over eighty years old, and although it is produced by those, and for those, who had little or no academic training, it still offers a scheme for the training of the ministry which would be difficult to improve."

With such an objective and methodology, Salvation Army training colleges are more like a turbulent battle-school than a sequestered seminary. Cadets must match the hours of the rooster and the owl. Not only must their brains be trained and tested, but their character and resourcefulness, too. One traditional way of doing this, popular with training college staff for several generations, is called "Personal Initiative."

On a given day in the district where they regularly conduct their practical and pastoral ministry, the cadets are asked to embark individually on an enterprise of their own design which, by its unusualness, will cause members of the public to be challenged by the Christian gospel message.

Cadet Norman Bearcroft heard of the intended adventure with a mixture of apprehension and gloom. Norman had entered the International Training College, London, in 1950 as a professional musician, having first been a member of His Majesty's Life Guard Regiment and then a freelance musician playing trumpet or French horn with London orchestras. As he heard fellow cadets telling of their intended wild schemes to arrest the attention of apathetic Londoners, his foreboding increased. Yet as a sincere evangelist himself, he wanted to play his part, but not in any foolish way. What could he do? He had no idea.

It was with a measure of relief, therefore, he listened to Cadet Chris Jorgensen, a Danish lad training at the International College. Chris suggested that he and Norman should pair up for this adventure. They should both board a London bus, Norman in full Army uniform, but Chris with his collar turned up and without his cap. They would go to the upper deck, Norman to a front seat but Chris remaining at the back. If there were a number of passengers up there with them, that would provide an audience for Chris to shout questions at the Army man and for Norman to witness to his faith in reply.

Norm was reluctant to agree. But what could he do? He had no bright ideas himself. Finally he said yes.

Feeling nervous and self-conscious, Cadet Bearcroft

boarded the bus and made his way to the very front seat of its top deck, followed by the incognito Cadet Jorgensen, who took the very back seat. Chris allowed a minute or two to pass, then he began:

"Hey, Salvation Army, why do you wear that funny uniform? What are you all dressed up like that for?"

Norman froze. His worst fears were being realized. He couldn't bring himself to shout back.

Chris tried again: "Salvation Army, I'm talking to you, what are you dressed up in that uniform for?"

A hot flush now began to creep up Norman's neck. This was awful. What could he do? He should never have agreed to this crazy idea.

From his back seat, Chris was puzzled. Norm was hanging this out too long. He was beginning to feel desperate. Once more he tried:

"HOY, SALVATION ARMY, CAN'T YOU HEAR ME? ARE YOU DEAF OR SOMETHING? I want to know why you're decked-up in that crazy uniform!"

Passengers began to put down their newspapers, stopped gazing idly out of the windows at the passing scene, and turned to the scene inside their bus. By now the bus conductor had arrived upstairs to collect the fares. He went first of all to the front seat and as he took Norman's fare he quietly asked, "Excuse me, sir, is that man at the back annoying you?"

Norman gulped. "Well, as a matter of fact, yes he is," he declared.

With four rapid strides the conductor moved to the back seat. "Off," he commanded, with finger outstretched, "I'm stopping the bus for you to get off. No one's allowed to create a disturbance. Off you go." Four rings of the bell brought the bus to an immediate halt.

In silence and open-mouthed, the Danish lad hurried down the stairs and hopped off the bus. Norman did not look behind to see if Chris was shaking his fist at him.

But the experience did nothing to deter Cadet Chris Jorgensen's eagerness to do the unusual. Norman Bearcroft found himself involved yet again in an embarrassing moment with him.

Both were appointed members of a campaign party sent to enlighten the dark souls of Middlesbrough, in the north of England. Chris was certain that normal open-air religious meetings would never arouse the interest of these hard-boiled northerners. So, when the campaigners next took up position on a street corner and began to sing, "We're bound for the land of the pure and the holy," there was Chris, in his best Danish suit, on the opposite side of the street, laughing at them.

Norman stepped forward into the ring of cadets and began to speak about his faith. "Rubbish," yelled Chris in his heavily accented English, "what a load of rubbish! Why don't you go and get yourselves a proper job instead of making that awful noise, disturbing honest citizens."

Chris was now enjoying the part of a heckler. He warmed to the task. There were no half measures about Chris. And there was no doubting that his declared intention of arousing interest was proving successful. A group of bystanders congregated.

Chris decided to get them on his side. "These Sally Army people regard you as sinners. Did you know that? They do. What right have they to come and say such things to you?"

The growing crowd began to murmur. Senior-Captain Gordon Cox decided things were getting a bit out of hand. He couldn't be seen talking personally to Chris, lest the crowd realized it was a ruse. So across the street he called, "That will do, my friend. You know we are here to offend no one."

But Chris decided that his leader was playing along with him. His abuse became all the stronger. There was now anger in his voice.

Then from the bystanders a broad-shouldered Middlesbrough working woman, with biceps that would have done credit to a dockyard navvy, shook her fist at the far smaller Chris. "You shut yer gob," she yelled. "We don't want yer sort coming over 'ere interfering. Get back to where you came from."

She strode over to Norman. "Don't you take any notice, love. You're doing yer best. We'll fix him when you've gone. You won't get any more trouble from him." The way she said "him" left none in doubt that the fate awaiting Chris if he stayed around was none too pleasant.

Senior-Captain Cox came to the rescue. "Sir," he called across to Chris, "why don't you come back with us to our citadel where we can talk things over with you? A man of such strong views must surely agree to that proposal."

"All right," responded the greatly relieved Chris. "I will come with you." And they marched him off with two of the larger cadets on either side of him, lest these Salvation Army supporters attack as he went.

<hr/>

The ten of us from the "Warriors" Session appointed to a ten-day evangelistic campaign at Cradley Heath in the industrial midlands of Britain knew from the outset that our campaign leader, Senior-Captain Geoffrey Dalziel, meant business. Even as we were alighting from the train at Birmingham New Street and making for the station exit, he called us, "Just a moment, cadets. Let us claim Cradley Heath for Christ right away."

He clustered us to him, removed his cap and addressed the Almighty in such stentorian tones that all the lesser mortals leaving the train could not help but hear also. We, too, doffed our caps and bowed our heads, more in shy defense than deference, I fear. "We claim liberty for the men and women of Cradley Heath who are bound in Satan's chains," he boomed—a nice touch, since Cradley was a center for industrial chain-making. I felt the hair bristle on the nape of my neck.

Each morning began with prayer at the citadel. Then off to door-to-door visitation. We became quite expert visitors. As we were about to leave a poverty-ridden home one morning, we both began to kneel down for prayer, then both stood up again instinctively. The floor was so dirty. Out in the street again, we were convulsed with laughter at our united reaction, synchronized as if rehearsed.

From across the road a man hailed us. "If I had your spirit I'd want to leave," we heard him say. We sobered up immediately. Was he criticizing us, we wondered? Did he somehow know about our refusing to kneel in that poor woman's house? "What do you mean, you'd want to leave?" we asked him. "I'd want to *leave* not *leave*," he responded. Suddenly light dawned. His midlands accent was deceiving us. He meant that if he had our spirit, he would want to *live*!

We took him to the citadel and learned his story. He was suicidal and without hope. We talked with him, fed him, prayed with him and in succeeding days helped him discover Christ as Lord. He became a vital part of our campaign. We thanked a mirthful God for using our crazy humor to help a hopeless man find joy.

＝

Two-hour Saturday night "raids" on Soho, the heart of London's night life, have been a nerve-racking challenge for Salvation Army officer-cadets at the Army's International Training College since first introduced in 1946 by Senior-Captain Geoffrey Dalziel. Tactics that will arrest the attention of the hordes of pleasure-seekers thronging the narrow streets to the message of the Christian gospel require courage and entrepreneurism of a high degree, not to mention both faith and prayer.

One week, the challenge became no easier when the small accordion being played by Cadet George Whittingham to accompany the group's earnest singing of hymns developed a fault. A note stuck and emitted a constant groaning.

"If I could just get the casing off," explained George to Senior-Captain Alf Holmes, the group leader, "I think I could repair it. I'll go into that pub over there and see if I can borrow some pliers."

Pushing his way through the over-crowded, noisy, smoke-filled bar, George spoke to the bar-tender: "Could you help me please? It's an unusual request. Do you have any pliers, please?"

"No, mate, sorry I can't help you," replied the Cockney barman. "I've got Marlborough, Craven A, Picadilly, Rothmans…but no Players. Sorry!"

All the cadets who arrived at London's International Training College by no means had had a thorough grounding in Old Testament history, their concentration having been mostly on the New Testament. But one young lady had been an ardent follower of the Salvation Army musicals written by the Gowans/Larsson duo and had been deeply impressed by the "Hosea" production. In Bible class on that prophetic book she raised her hand and challenged the teacher, "Why is there no reference to Light-Fingered Freddy?"

— *Iris Port.*

At a 1972 regional Salvation Army congress in Edmonton, Alberta, a Salvationist historian read anecdotes from the early history of the Army in Canada, including quotations from *The War Cry* prior to 1900. They included editorial answers to questions posed to the editor. Only the answers were given, not the questions. One answer was directed to a cadet, then in training. In its entirety it read, "No, cadet, there is nothing in Salvation Army regulations to prevent you becoming General."

— *Ernest A. Miller.*

It has become a tradition for the Army's General to give cadet training sessions a name which suggests a quality which would be the hallmark of these future officers. Some of the names chosen suggest those asked by the General to help choose a name had had quite a struggle themselves.

The 1930-31 session trained in New York was called "The

15

Climbers." It proudly rejoiced in having an all-women's brass band. Ruth Aitken was its sousaphone player, and reveled in her music-making, particularly when marching the streets proudly behind the gospel banner.

Positioned on the far right of the marching host, behind the college flags and staff, she would by conscious effort keep her eyes glued to the music, eager to play every note with precise accuracy, as though the advancement of the Christian cause rested entirely on her.

Thus she marched one evening along West 14th Street toward 8th Avenue subway station. Suddenly, totally without warning, *she dropped out of sight.* Someone on that pot-holed New York street had removed a manhole cover. Incredibly, those marching ahead of her and those following simply walked around the gaping hole, all seemingly more intent on continuing to do their bounden duty than to rescue Cadet Aitken.

Major Helen Purviance, of the college staff, along with an onlooker, found her clinging for dear life to her sousaphone. The large bell had remained above ground and saved her from being washed down to the Hudson River. She needed a new coat and spectacles, but otherwise the enthusiastic sousaphonist was OK.

It certainly helped print the name of her session indelibly on her mind—a "Climber" indeed.

~~~

Individual counseling of cadets by officer-staff is given a high priority in the training program. The "P.I."—personal interview—is either welcomed, tolerated or feared by the cadets, according to the reputation of the interviewer.

One lad, somewhat naive, was being interviewed by the rosy cheeked, smiling Senior-Captain Gordon Cox.

"You know what your trouble is, don't you?" he asked the young cadet.

"No, sir, I don't," he replied, wide-eyed.

"Well, you're too demure, reserved, shy; too inhibited; a bit of an unjustified inferiority complex, I suspect."

"Oh, I see, sir. Thank you, sir, for telling me.'"

A week later the same lad was instructed to report to Major John Moyse for another P.I. It was proceeding pleasantly enough, then Major Moyse asked, "You know what you're trouble is, don't you, cadet?"

"Yes, sir, I do," replied the lad.

"You do?" said the Major in some astonishment.

"Yes, I'm too demure, reserved and shy. I've got a bit of an unjustified inferiority…"

"Nonsense," cut in the astounded Major Moyse. *"It's the Devil telling you that."*

The first full-term session of training for both men and women cadets in Britain after World War II was called, appropriately enough, the "Warriors" session. In September 1946, 220 women and 97 men, products of the war years, arrived at the Denmark Hill college—itself battle-scarred after having survived a land mine dropped by parachute on a nearby public house called "The Fox on the Hill" (afterwards renamed "The Fox under the Hill" by the landlord).

Nearly all the men cadets arrived straight from navy, army, or air force duty. They presented new problems for a faculty which had not handled cadets who had battled U-boats in the Atlantic, swept Rommel out of Africa, been in D-Day Normandy landings and flown the first faster-than-sound jets over Germany.

Having been delayed from entering the college throughout the six years of war, many of the men were older than the normal pre-war intake. One man, Wally Holiday, would bemoan his prospects for promotion, declaring that he knew the Army would never elect to have a General Holiday.

Food rationing continued for Britain during the immediate post-war years. Cadets, whose youthful appetites had been well satisfied with abundant servicemen's rations, were now on civilian rations and constantly hungry. There was one potato per day, cooked in its jacket. (The jacket was eaten, too. Had there been a waistcoat, that also would have been devoured.) A small weekly portion of butter and sugar was given each cadet to take by dish and tin each mealtime to the dining hall, often never to arrive intact, a calamity greeted with ribald cheers as the unfortunate's dish smashed on the concrete pathway. The remainder of the ration was kept by the college chef for general cooking purposes.

Inevitably, there was a rush back to houses between classes to brew tea, coffee, cocoa. If any dear pal had received a food parcel sacrificially sent by loved ones, it was felt to be the duty of his friends to help him demolish the goodies. In consequence, wolfish cadets often arrived late for the succeeding class and lectures. Not surprisingly, the Training Principal (Australian Commissioner John S. Bladin), took a poor view of lads, well-trained in military undercover operations, unsuccessfully trying to creep unseen into the assembly hall while he was offering his pearls of wisdom.

So it was decreed that there should be a roll call, some minutes earlier than the lecture, outside the assembly hall before any lecture by the Commissioner. Cadet Sergeant- Major John Elsworth would conduct this discipline. The precious minutes for appeasing hunger would therefore be fewer still.

When the Sergeant-Major took up position outside the assembly hall, an astonishing sight met his eyes. Advancing toward him along the top avenue was the almost entire cadet body of 300 marching men and women, fully uniformed and led by the flags and 30-piece band. They played and sang exuberantly "When the roll is called up yonder, I'll be there."

But, as the Sergeant-Major saw, they didn't stay there. They swept past him, all round the college grounds. There was no lecture that day. No roll calls were ever suggested again. The fact that the Army's International Headquarters top brass (then quartered at the college because their headquarters had been blitzed on May 8, 1941) had witnessed the protest march could have played a part in canceling the order. Which hungry cadet organized the protest? The identity remains a mystery.

≈≈

Salvation Army officers remember their cadet training days in vivid detail. They all believe their training session was unique, comprising personalities who did things no cadet had ever done, who said things no cadet had ever said. No matter how advanced in years, the most veteran officer will relate, "Why, in my session we had a cadet who went up to the Chief Side Officer and said…" Session reunions to mark the twenty-fifth, thirtieth, fortieth, fiftieth even sixtieth commissioning anniversaries will resonate with endless stories usually beginning, "Remember when old Charlie Bloggs climbed up the drainpipe of House 5…."

Here are some of former Cadet Stanley Richardson's memories:

Every cadet was required to produce a new sermon outline each fortnight. One of our company was completely lacking in inspiration. The outline had to be handed in on time at all costs. A sympathetic fellow cadet came to the rescue with a book, *One Hundred Best Sermons,* by the famous preacher Charles Haddon Spurgeon. With great relief, the worried cadet made an outline of one that suited the method under instruction.

It came back from the education officer with the terse comment: "Not up to your usual standard."

≈≈

Officers and cadet-sergeants from the International Training College had invaded a south coast seaside resort. Our over-enthusiasm was probably a cloak for our nervousness. At any rate, it was not appreciated by some of the holiday-makers wanting quietly to relax on the promenade. "I'll never give another farthing to The Salvation Army," exclaimed a lady with a very lah-di-dah upper class accent.

Major Harry Warren, the Field Training Officer, turned and from what must have seemed a great height to the reclining lady boomed in his deep voice, "Madam, do you usually only give farthings to The Salvation Army?"

The Scandinavian cadet was very worried when he saw his name on the program for the first weekend services at the corps which was to be our out-training center. He was asked to tell about his own Christian experience and faith. He explained to the house officer that his command of the English language was not yet up to the standard for public speaking.

The captain had a bright idea to help the nervous cadet. He suggested that the Scandinavian lad should play some gospel music on his accordion and then "Just say a few words."

The meeting arrived all too quickly for the cadet. He played his accordion and then began to speak:

"Zee accordion is a very vunderful instrument. There are zee reeds, and zee tubes and zee keys. There are zee bellows and when I squeeze zee bellows, I press zee key, so! Zee vind goes through zee tubes and zee reeds and plays zee notes. Zee instrument is very vunderful but without zee vind there would be no music. My friends, do you have zee vind?"

Former-cadet Houston Ellis, of Atlanta, Georgia, USA, also has his memories:

A cadet was lining out the last verse of the old Richard Jukes hymn during an open-air meeting. He earnestly declared:

"My old companions, fare you well,
To hell with you, I will not go."

It was another cadet who, for added effect, was making many dramatic gestures as he outlined a song in another open-air meeting. He pointed upward as he read: "When the roll is called up yonder" He pointed downward as he concluded, "I'll be there."

During a jail meeting, a cadet was asked to sing a solo. He talked for a few minutes and expressed astonishment that he had been asked to sing. But then he added: "I just happen to have this song in my pocket."

The young cadet leading a meeting for which he and fellow cadets were responsible decided that enough was enough and wanted to get back to the training college. He announced, "I feel that the Lord is leading me now to close the meeting." Whereupon the brigade officer stood up and stated, "That is strange, cadet. The Lord is telling me to lead another song."

A brigade of women cadets, conducting a springtime evangelical campaign, had finally become quite outdone (i.e. fed up) with the demands of their brigade officer. In an open-air meeting, the officer turned to one and commanded, "Now, cadet, you fire a gospel shot" (i.e. declaim a Scripture text). The young lady, who in later years became a distinguished territorial officer, stepped forward, pointed one finger at the audience and yelled, "BANG!" Needless to say, the brigade officer did not think this funny—but then, brigade officers are funny that way. Unlike the makeshift pistol, the exasperated cadet was not fired, but she was hauled over the coals.

Eight cadet-sergeants—commissioned from the "Warriors" session to help in the training of the succeeding "King's Messengers" session—were conducting a two-week summer evangelistic campaign in the Southampton and Channels Isles Division, a regular annual fixture in between cadet-training sessions. Adjutant Geoffrey Dalziel and Captain Howard Orsborn were the campaign leaders.

Most mornings provided free time. Afternoons were devoted to beach meetings with an emphasis on attracting children. Well-advertised public rallies attracted scores of people in the evening. The concluding high spot of these was the enactment of a Scriptural drama about the imprisoned St. Paul and Onesimus, the converted slave. Since the campaign moved on each day to a new coastal resort, a great deal of improvisation was needed for the "stage" props. Audiences were told it would challenge their imagination in the finest traditions of English theater.

The part of the Roman soldier guarding the imprisoned Paul was played by Leslie Pull, a natural piece of casting since he was 6' 2", broad of shoulder and deep-voiced. It was always a telling moment when Les entered, threw himself on a couch or whatever piece of furniture the local Salvationists had been able to provide, and began to tell how intrigued he had become with the unusual prisoner he was guarding. This was a very safe and quite moving part of the play.

At Southsea, where the Salvation Army hall's platform rises steeply in tiers to become level at its topmost with the gallery—in the style of the old-fashioned music-halls—the only kind of "couch" available for Les was a type of folding stretcher, but with unusually high legs. Les declared it to be fully satisfactory for his moving performance.

With his customary words, "How wearying this day has been and how perplexed I am about this prisoner…" Les entered. But this night, to add emphasis to his weariness and anxiety, he removed his large brass Roman soldier helmet with a flourish and placed it *upside down under the high stretcher* before stretching his lengthy body out on it.

To the hundreds in the audience, the Roman helmet was suddenly transformed into one of the most humble of all domestic utensils, a chamber pot. A roar of laughter broke out. Each time it began to subside, a fresh wave of guffaws swept the building. And each time Les began to recite, "How wearying this day has been…" it was a signal for yet more howls of merriment.

The reaction of those attending: "The best evangelical meeting I've ever been to."

~

Cadet-Sergeant Frank Davies, responsible for the training of "Warriors" cadets in youth and young people's work at Shepherd's Bush, West London, was becoming increasingly irritated by the mad dash of his charges to a local cafe the moment an evening meeting ended.

"It's not right, fellers," he declared with unusual severity. "It's our job to shake hands with people after a meeting, bid them a good-night and a 'God bless you,' then make for the bus stop so we can all get back to college as soon as we can. You can't be all that hungry, anyway."

For once the cadets didn't protest, though they disagreed about not being hungry. That night, they hurried meekly along to the bus stop, yielding not to the temptation of the cafe en route.

They had all left the hall by the time Frank got away. He wondered if his words had had any effect. Just to be sure, he peered on tiptoes over the top of the brass-railed green curtain which filled the lower two-thirds of the cafe window. Frank could hardly believe his eyes. There, wearing their caps were four uniformed figures, their backs to the window. Anger filled him as he blazed into the cafe.

"Look, you fellers, this is too much..." He suddenly spluttered to a stop. "Oh, I beg your pardon, gentlemen. Your bus inspectors' uniform is so much like ours. I mistook you. So sorry. Good night!"

The War Cry, the pugilistic title given to the main periodical published by The Salvation Army in each of its territories, has become by tradition a valuable weekly point of contact between Salvationists and their customers. For the Army salespersons—called pub-boomers when the point of sale is the pub or liquor store—the weekly round can be quite an adventure, as Canadian Captain John Moore relates:

I'll never forget my summer appointment as a cadet, for it was there in Chatham, Ontario, that I learned to dance.

Three or four stalwarts and I would do the Friday night pub ministry. Our last call, about 11:30 p.m., was always at the Royal Canadian Legion Branch. Usually, the Legionnaires were delighted to see us and everything came to a standstill when the master of ceremonies announced, "The Sally Ann's here, folks. Dig deep!"

My last Friday night will live forever in the annals of the grand old Chatham Citadel, the number 4 corps in Canada. That night, emerging drenched from one of those torrential rainstorms that suddenly hit southwestern Ontario and then just as suddenly pass over, my companion and I entered the Legion hall. Somehow I knew that this night was going to be...well, different.

The air was heavy, the heat oppressive, the Legionnaires and their ladies were slicked with sweat, and all of them half-boiled, it seemed. Particularly the large, buxom, bottle- blonde, tugboat Annie type, a three-sheets-to-the-wind lady who took an immediate fancy to Cadet Moore. I fended her off with as much grace as a wet cadet was capable of mustering. "Have a *War Cry*," said I, grinning tightly and proffering the little red collecting box, more as a defense than an opening ploy.

Sweeping the box and *War Cry* aside with one swipe of her beefy arm, tugboat Annie froze me with a headlock that was paralyzing. She wrapped her other formidable arm around my waist and wrestled me to the center of the dance floor, where the other revelers hastily cleared a large space. I think they'd seen her in action before.

Yanking my head back, she leered bleerily in my face and croaked, "Dance, kid, or I'll break your arm!" As the insistent, low, throbbing beat of "Hernando's Hideaway" filled the steamy, smoke-filled air, she pushed, jerked and man-handled me all over the dance floor, to the wild applause of the gathered, lathered gentry of Chatham, and to the unmitigated joy of my fellow pub-boomers.

And that's how I learned to do the tango.

CHAPTER 3

THE PRINTER MEANT
NO HARM

MEMBERS OF SALVATION ARMY editorial departments, and all who have close association with the printing trade, tend to harbor suspicions that not all "typos" and misprints that escape correction are accidental. A witty employee, bored by routine, may find it hard to resist the temptation to liven up the day by creating a "howler" in a journal with a simple one-letter alteration.

Funnier still, sometimes, are the "howlers" which an eager but somewhat unsophisticated correspondent will commit in rushing off his "masterpiece" to gain some inches about local events.

Lieut.-Colonel Eric Coward, former Editor of the London *War Cry* and then Editor-in-Chief in Canada, where he retired, made a collection of humorous misprints and of quotes from reports submitted by correspondents. The following are from his "treasure trove."

"Before laying down the baton for the last time, the retiring songster leader conducted the brigade through "Now I am Free."

"Though still in poor health, the bandmaster was able to conduct the band in two pieces."

"Commissioner Gordon Simpson has had an operation. He is expecting another son (soon)."

—*Atlanta War Cry*

"Mrs. Nancy Rathbone of the Mountain Mission shows interested Home Leaguers how to put a bottom in a chair."

—*Photo caption in Atlanta War Cry*.

"Greenhow, Eric. Born September 21, 1904.………Butcher, but enjoyed cooking. Portion of finger missing on left hand."

—*Missing Persons Dept. advertisement*

"The opening song at the retirement of the Commissioner was, "O Happy, Happy Day when Old Things Passed Away.""

"Sister Mrs. Penney has been promoted to Glory (Army terminology for dying). She was our champion collector. Her passing has left the town a poorer place."

"The Army's capacity for disaster has been recognized by the U.S. Senate."

"Why not accept a career in the British Red Shield

Services for spiritually-minded people with no children?"

＝＝

"As his body was lowered into the grave, the songsters sang his favorite chorus, 'Just where He needs me, my Lord has placed me'."

＝＝

"We had special services in connection with Liberation Day. It was farewell Sunday for Major and Mrs. Potter."

＝＝

"A backslider left his cigarettes at the Mercy Seat, to the joy of his comrades."

＝＝

"During the past six weeks God has been with us. On Sunday the Divisional Commander was with us."

＝＝

"After hearing Bandsman Davy's cornet solo, a young woman offered for China."

＝＝

"The band visited the hospital to play to the mayor. He is now recovering."

＝＝

"Major and Mrs. George Clark dispensed lively beat music with the aid of guitars and amplifiers and soon got the children singing, 'Whisper a prayer in the morning'."

＝＝

"A soldier prayed, 'Lord, kindle a fire in her heart and pour water upon it, that she may bring forth fruit'."

"Lord, bless our leaders and show them the way out."

"We mean to serve God to the bitter end."

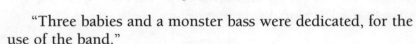

"The high spot of the evening was the way the retired bandmaster handled his bass. Although he has not played for some years, his execution brought forth a round of applause."

"Following a traffic accident, a heavenly summons came to Bandsman Charlie Speed."

"Three babies and a monster bass were dedicated, for the use of the band."

" She was a lifelong reader of *The War Cry* and bore suffering with great fortitude."

"On Sunday we had a combined memorial service for Brother Billings and H.M. the King."

"The band gave a festival of praise which was held in connection with the farewell of our officers."

"Congress Sunday was hell (held) at Newcastle."

"The General was met by a large crow (crowd) singing 'Glory, hallelujah'."

"His retirement certificate was singed (signed) by the Divisional Commander."

"In her last illness she loved to talk about her long association with the cops (corps)."

"…most of the older families had moved father (farther) out into the country."

"The chairman was Bandsman R. Rearden and the yell-balanced program included 'Born to be King' and the 'Hallelujah' Chorus."

"I was to meet the bandmaster many times when he visited Govan to conduct the annual bad weekend."

"Thanks to the kind offices of one of our comrades, who has attended the band practices with his ape recorder…"

"As they now hopefully turn their backs on the freezing winds and lark evenings, enthusiastic open-air…"

A funeral program was being printed. One of the songs

incorporated in the service was, "There is a better world, they say." Printing had to be quickly stopped when the machine operator noticed that line 6 of verse 1 read, "Angels with bright WIGS are there." That was one that nearly got away.

—*Fred Norton, for many years in the composing room at the Army's Campfield Press, St. Albans.*

QUOTES FROM THE PAPERS and circulars, provided by the Rev. John R. Mowat:

"Songster Mrs. Kirkham sang the first verse and then the congregation all sank together."

"Come in your thousands. The Congress Hall seats 900."

"Great trouser offer....every pain guaranteed."

"During a recent band league tea, the Band Secretary was admitted to hospital suffering from buns."

"Quiet, clean Salvationist seeks comfortable room where he can cook himself on a spirit stove."

CHAPTER 4

SING UNTO THE LORD WITH TRUMPETS AND VOICE

F ROM ITS EARLIEST DAYS THE SALVATION ARMY seems to have taken the instructions in Psalm 98 quite literally. Salvationists have never had any inhibitions about "making a joyful noise unto the Lord," as many a late lie-a-bed on a Sunday morning has discovered when their street has been invaded for what Salvationists call "open-air witness." Not often have they sung "unto the Lord with the harp" (though they plan to make amends when St. Peter allows them through the pearly gates), but they would contend that the man who urged "With trumpets and sound of cornet make a joyful noise before the Lord," had all the makings of a fine Salvation Army bandsman.

Victorians who loved their music halls were fascinated when a Salvation Army with brass and drums burst in on the dignified nineteenth century ecclesiastical scene. They cheerfully joined in when the Salvationists adapted their favorite

"Champagne Charlie Is Me Name" to words that told of their conversion: "Bless His Name, He Sets Me Free."

Many of today's bands and songster brigades attain standards of excellence comparable to professional groups, though the members are all unpaid amateurs, motivated still by the injunction, "Make a joyful noise unto the Lord." They still take to heart the instruction of their Founder, William Booth: "Sing the simple old truths in the simple old hearty way that God has already blessed so widely in the salvation of souls."

And in the singing and playing of those simple old truths, whether it be in Buckingham Palace forecourt or in the dingiest back-street slum, these musical messengers enjoy marvelous fellowship, have joy in their hearts and, often enough—intentionally or unintentionally—moments of rollicking good humor.

The commitment to street ministry is very strong among many of the Army's bandmasters. The Army began on the streets in the East End of London in 1865 and has never lost the conviction that it remains the church of the pavement. Some have called its bands the Army's peripatetic organ.

Lt.-Colonel Norman Bearcroft, composer, conductor and organizer of major musical events, certainly relishes marches and meetings on the streets. That was evident to me when in the 1970s I called on him during a visit to Canada where for seven years he was head of the music department and had formed the Canadian Staff Band—a re-forming, actually, since the original staff band had perished when the *Empress of Ireland* sank in 1914.

I was immediately invited to accompany the staff band for a weekend of events at Orillia, Ontario. When I first heard the town's name I thought it must be spelled like the tune to which we sing the hymn, "From Greenland's Icy Mountains" as well it might have been since the snow was piled six feet high on either side of the roads.

But the sun shone brightly from an azure sky on Sunday morning, enough to convince Bandmaster Bearcroft that the band could march (or glide) to play to patients at the local hospital. It meant playing non-stop to prevent valves and slides from freezing in the sub-zero temperature.

Open-air meetings are not held regularly on Sunday mornings in Canada, there being a fine system of adult Bible classes held in Sunday school. But Norman argued that open-air meetings were a requirement of international Orders and Regulations, a favorite argument he used effectively about several matters. Since he was a top man from London and therefore should know, his bandsmen acquiesced. Besides, they liked him.

As a visitor, I was accorded a place behind the Flag Sergeant for the return march from the hospital, flanked by Norman and the band's Executive Officer. The double-tap of the drum to signal the march commencement had scarcely sounded when a mongrel dog positioned itself in front of me immediately behind the Flag Sergeant. Its nose hovered over the flag man's shoes, as though he had cleaned them with meat paste instead of cherry blossom. Its tail drooped. It did not seem to be a happy tyke. No amount of shooing or "Get aht of it" affected the mutt. On it followed.

But as we approached the T-junction road ahead, it suddenly darted forward and turned to face the band, placing itself centrally with paws astride, as though controlling the traffic. When the band had marched past, it scurried back to take up its position behind the Flag Sergeant again. Nose to his shoes, tail still drooping, there was no display of pride in its achievement.

As the next turning came in sight, we wondered what our faithful hound would do. To our delight, it repeated its performance exactly and did so yet once more, at the last turning before we arrived back at the citadel. Thirty Canadian Staff bandsmen can testify to the accuracy of my tale!

I have never given any credence to the idea of reincarnation. It's ridiculous to imagine that any former Salvation Army Corps Sergeant-Major's traffic-controlling spirit had taken up residence in a four-footed friend—though haven't I seen that haunting, hang-dog look on the faces of burdened local officers at some corps?

NORMAN'S ARGUMENT, "It's in international Orders and Regulations," was heard again when the Canadian Staff Band visited Winnipeg, Manitoba. The Sunday morning open-air meeting had been held and the bandsmen were preparing to stroll or be taken by car back to the citadel.

"Surely we're going to march?" questioned Bandmaster Bearcroft.

"No, I'm sorry," said the Divisional Commander, a Lieut.-Colonel. "We have to have police permission and have an escort to march in this city, something we have to apply for at least two weeks in advance."

"Surely not," responded Norman with some passion. "This is a sacred right for which our forebears fought and even died. We must not let go the right which cost them so much. It's in international Orders and Regulations that we should march." In a tone which made plain that the discussion was over, Major Bearcroft announced, "Right, gentlemen, let's form up for the march back."

With colors flying proudly, the band set forth. The hymn tune sounded glorious in the still morning air. Then came another sound, less glorious, overriding even the band's playing. The screams of police sirens. Stepping from his car, the police officer strode straight to Norman at the head of the march. "Are you in charge of this march?" he demanded.

"Actually, no," replied Bandmaster Bearcroft, "he is," pointing to the Colonel.

Without comment, the Colonel was hustled into the police car. The band disbanded. The indoor morning service was almost over before the Divisional Commander rejoined his subdued, law-breaking comrades. On his face was the expression of a man who would not again be impressed by the argument about international Orders and Regulations.

AS DEPUTY BANDMASTER of the small band at Welling, a suburb of London, I was on duty in the absence of the bandmaster for a Sunday night meeting to be led by Major Fred Biggs, the former International Staff Band flag officer who had passed on his beloved banner to unworthy me. His appointment to the Army's International Audit Department had robbed him of proudly holding aloft the Staff Band colors. As auditor he had to travel overseas for weeks at a time.

Fred had just returned from inspecting the Army's finances in the Netherlands, hence the C.O.'s invitation for him to lead the meeting. He came into the band room where we bandsmen were preparing for the service and announced in an excited way that he wanted our help. "You see," he explained, "wherever I go overseas, the Salvationists seem so happy, so joyful. But back home here, everyone is so stiff, so starchy with a 'Bless me if you can' attitude. Tonight the theme of the meeting is 'JOY!' and I need your help." We listened as Fred outlined his plan.

During his sermon on JOY, he would suddenly exclaim, "THIS JOY: WHO'S GOT IT?" whereupon he would want the baritone and euphonium players to sing, "I have" on the notes of lower E and C, and then to sustain that C. The tenor horn players would at once sing "I have" on G and E notes, likewise holding the E. Then back row cornets would also sing "I have" on notes C and G. Finally, front row cornets would sing "I have" on notes E and C. Then from the full harmonious chord thus formed we would break into the rollicking Army chorus, "I've got the joy, joy, joy, joy, down in my heart." That, Fred was convinced, would really stir up these stern sober Britishers.

This sober Britisher admitted to having a little apprehension about such an unrehearsed venture. Like the disciples of old, we looked for a sign. Could Fred give us a clear indication when he wanted the baritone and euphonium to commence? Fred was immediately the essence of helpfulness. "Of course," he responded warmly, "I'll put out my arm like this (he gestured dramatically) as I ask, 'Who's got it?'"

I shrugged and agreed. We took our places on the platform. The meeting proceeded smoothly, I reminding myself to stay awake and pay attention.

Fred was in good form—lively, energetic in style, vigorous. He was holding the attention of the congregation with a description of the Army's practical service in Holland —this well before his actual sermon—when the baritone player suddenly emitted in a weak quivery baa-lamb voice, "I have." The startled euphonium player was jolted into joining him for the last part of the "have." The tenor horns woke up. Totally out of key, they offered their "I have." Back row cornets leapt on different notes for their contribution. On the front row, we too could achieve no harmony. At least half an octave lower than the proper pitch, we droned through the "Joy, joy, joy" chorus. The effusive joy drained from Fred's face. Had it been a funeral dirge it could not have sounded more somber.

Fred and I remained good friends, but he never again spoke to me about the stiff starchiness of the British.

＿～＿

IN THE ARMY WE TEND TO LIONIZE our music composers, arrangers and performers. The names of previous generals may not stay on our lips, but those of our composers are indelibly engraved. The living are held in some awe.

As a lieutenant, newly appointed to the Army's UK headquarters after only a short term as a Corps Officer, Ray Bowes was asked to compose a fanfare. Played by a group of teenage bandsmen, it would give a vigorous commencement to a great youth meeting at Regent Hall, Oxford Street, in the heart of London's West End. Lieutenant Bowes was then to tell the distinguished Major Charles Skinner, a famous composer indeed and the bandmaster of the Regent Hall Band, what key he had chosen for his fanfare. Major Skinner would thus be able to select a march in the same key for his band to accompany the rousing march into the hall of the youthful delegates.

Lieutenant Bowes knew Major Skinner only by repute. On the day of the youth congress he looked for him. He espied the tall, dignified bandmaster among a group of chatting colleagues. With deference he approached the great man.

"Excuse me, Bandmaster," he said, looking up into the impassive features, "but my fanfare is in the key of E flat."

Charles Skinner's face showed no emotion. He had no idea who the lieutenant was or why he was passing on this jewel of information. The youth rally organizer had forgotten to tell him of the plan.

After a moment of silence he intoned, "How intriguing!"

For years afterwards, as they became the closest of colleagues, Charles and Ray would greet each other with, "How intriguing!"

THE SAME MAJOR SKINNER was to feature in an important composers' night festival at Regent Hall with fellow composer Bandmaster Herbert Mountain, formerly of Sheffield Citadel but now of Blackpool Citadel. A great deal of additional interest had been aroused by the organizer's success in persuading Stuart Hibberd to be the compere.

Every home throughout Britain knew Stuart Hibberd's velvet voice for he was the BBC's chief news reader. During war days especially, millions of radios at home and overseas would be tuned to the BBC's nightly 9 o'clock news. Somehow, even amidst the terrors of nightly Luftwaffe bombing over London, his voice indicated there was no cause for alarm.

Before the music festival commenced, Mr. Hibberd met the two composers, the tall Charles Skinner and the short, stocky Herbert Mountain.

"This is Bandmaster Skinner and this is Bandmaster Mountain," said the introducer.

The familiar mellifluous silken voice filled the room, as

though from a radio. Turning to Charles Skinner, the distinguished BBC man commented, "You know, I would have thought you were Bandmaster Mountain by reason of your height."

Just how highly Bandmaster Mountain was esteemed was well demonstrated by Bandsman Gresty, of Leith, Scotland, who answered an advertisement in *The Musician* for a trombone player. The advert did not mention that the vacancy existed in Blackpool, where Herbert Mountain had become the corps' bandmaster.

Wanting to list his qualifications, Bandsman Gresty wrote: "I have played in Sheffield Citadel Band under Bandmaster Herbert Mountain —*the* Herbert Mountain."

He received a reply from Blackpool signed, "Herbert Mountain—*the* Herbert Mountain."

OF COURSE, " 'T AINT WHAT YER SAY" it's the occasion when you say it that can make it memorable or not. For example, in 1941 the International Staff Band was commanded to play in the forecourt of Buckingham Palace, an honor to mark its golden jubilee. The bandsmen learned in advance that some of them might be personally introduced to HM King George VI.

Ray Wiggins tells me that side-drummer Arthur Bisshopp dared privately to wonder if he might be one of the privileged few and, if so, what he might say. He guessed that the King might ask him how long he had been a Salvationist and so he prepared his reply.

Unfortunately for Arthur, His Majesty inquired how long he had been a member of the Staff Band. "Ever since I was a baby, your majesty," replied Arthur automatically—and for several days afterward mentally kicked himself harder than he ever thwacked his drum.

ONE OF THE REASONS for a marching band having

percussionists became suddenly clear to a somewhat naive songster brigade member during a Sunday evening march from the open-air meeting back to Sheffield Citadel. Songster Mary Butcher pointed out to Songster Dorothy Hampshire that she was not in step.

Dorothy admitted the difficulty she found in keeping in step. The helpful Mary explained that all she had to do was to put her left foot down when Eddie Ducker banged his drum.

"D'ye know, love," said Dorothy, "I've often wondered why Eddie kept banging the drum when the band was not playing!"

—*Ray Wiggins.*

BECAUSE BANDS AND CHORAL GROUPS are always in the public eye, the need for a capable and confident public speaker to present their programs is paramount. But the most able can err. Songster Leader Fred Crowhurst was compering his songster brigade's program given to disabled club members. He introduced each item with great style, telling something about the composer and music. When it came to "Banners and Bonnets," he graphically described the profound regard for the Army which had moved writer Meredith Wilson to dedicate his song to the Movement and how well it captured the spirit and enthusiasm of the Army. "So," he concluded, "here is "Bonners and Bannets.""

The bandmaster at Caterham introduced some originality into his program by inviting each member of the band to introduce an item. A lady member did so most eloquently when her turn came, ending, "Now we will play for you 'The Rolid Sock'."

The Songster Leader in the small corps of Tenby, Wales, proudly announced some music by the masters, in fact, a song by Sherbert. "That will make a lovely fizz," cried a voice from the audience.

KNOWN FOR HIS SUCCESSFUL EVANGELISM, Major Henry Arrowood was invited to conduct a week of evangelistic services at Lexington, North Carolina. He was delighted to learn that in one meeting he would have the services of some local musicians calling themselves "The First Blue-Grass Gospel Group."

They gave themselves to their music with enthusiasm, and interspersed each item with an earnest sermonette. When it was the turn of the banjo player to speak, he softly strummed the strings and crooned in his Appalachian brogue: "Ma friends, the Lord has been speaking some very precious words to ma heart, but the three most precious words of all have been these:"

With a gasp and a stroke of the strings between each, the banjoist revealed all three: "I - FOR - GIVE."

ORGANIZERS ARE NOT ALWAYS AS CAREFUL at proof-reading their printed programs as they need to be. Major Joy Webb's fine composition, "Share my Yoke" suffers badly. At Boscombe, Bournemouth, England, cornet soloist Sheridan Bartlett evidently played "Share my Yolk," though there is nothing to suggest that the bandmaster egged him on or the audience egged him off. Commissioner Robert E. Thomson tells me that on a Sunday morning at West Palm Beach, Florida, the corps band presented "Share my Joke." No doubt it was hilarious!

Joy, founder of the Army's incredibly successful '60s "Joy Strings" pop group, would not have appreciated the mistake of a managing director in Newark, Nottinghamshire, when called on for financial support by Major Cliff Kent, a public relations officer. "I'm not a fan of your brass bands," he told Cliff, "but I loved your pop group. Weren't they called the *G -Strings*?"

OUTDOOR AUDIENCES can be even more critical of speakers than indoor congregations. Brigadier John Hunter recalls that in Bridgeport, Connecticut, the drummer was called on to speak about his Christian faith and experience in a Sunday evening open-air meeting. A rather shy and soft-spoken person, he was not helped when a lady of considerable proportions edged closer to the street curb with her hand cupped around an ear and called at the top of her voice, "Speak up, brother, even the devil can't hear what you're saying."

THEIR PROMINENT ROLE in worship and street ministry inevitably sculptures some music section leaders into intriguing personalities. They develop their own clearly identifiable gestures and mannerisms. They quickly discover the value of being known for having a ready wit and an ability to match any wags in band-room or rehearsal-time repartee.

Bandmaster Don Jenkins, of the outstanding Bristol Easton Band, England, fairly dances before his men, coaxing, caressing, softening or advancing the sounds from his musicians. He will even cease conducting, allowing the band to play on while he listens with evident rapture, as though to ask why his gymnastics should deny him the audio delights the audience is receiving. He describes such measures as "putting the band on automatic pilot."

When Commissioner Caughey Gauntlett, Chief of the Staff and second-in-command of the entire international Salvation Army, visited Bristol Easton Corps to conduct weekend meetings, Bandmaster Jenkins graciously offered the baton to the Commissioner in the Sunday morning open-air meeting. He knew that this top brass hat had been a keen euphoniumist in his younger days and would appreciate the opportunity of conducting such a group. What piece would he like to conduct? The Commissioner chose one of his favorites.

Some while later, the Commissioner's private secretary met Don and mentioned how thrilled his boss had been to conduct such a first-class band. "I knew he would be all right," commented Don. "But in any case, the band was on automatic pilot."

THE NAME OF BANDMASTER ALF SPRINGATE lives on in Salvation Army brass band circles, largely because of his dedication to the cause of training young musicians. Being a schoolmaster by profession and having a delicious—and at times wickedly penetrating—sense of humor, he was an ideal senior member of staff at Salvation Army National Schools of Music in Britain.

Where more sedate authoritarian staff members would fail to win the willing co-operation of reluctant young men, Alf's wit and wisdom gained their instant laughing response. For instance, when a school photograph was to be taken after lunch, the hired photographer needed several large tables taken outdoors, and he asked Alf to make the announcement.

Poker-faced, Alf announced, "Would all the corner-men soloists of each band, please stand." They proudly stood, imagining they had won some new accolade. "Thank you, lads. I'd like each one of you corner-men to grab a corner of these tables and carry them outside, please." Cheers from all the lesser mortals.

The Salvation Army itself was having to grow up and out of its narrow thinking about youth in those days. Alf was a good teacher. When some of the hierarchy insisted that all recreation should be kept out of Sundays at the music school, Alf was unsparing in his debunking.

Finally carrying the reluctant judgment of some brass hats, he stood to address the two hundred young teenagers one scorching Sunday lunch-time:

"Boys, permission has been given to use the swimming pool between sessions." When the cheers had died down he

Booth is lampooned in the "St. Stephen's Review," February 20, 1882. The satire is now on sale as a postcard, copyrighted in 1990, by Salvationist Publishing and Supplies Ltd. (What in heaven does William think of that!)

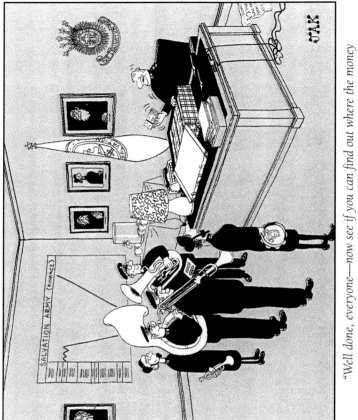

"Well done, everyone—now see if you can find out where the money went from Barings!"

When General Paul Rader held a press conference to announce the recovery of the missing millions stolen from the Army in the U.K., artist JAK joined in the rejoicings with this cartoon in London's *Evening Standard*. He quipped that the intrepid Salvationist sleuths might now help Barings, London's oldest merchant bank, trace the huge sums they lost in Singapore. Reproduction by kind permission of Solo Syndication Limited.

Cartoonist BROOK in Britain's *Daily Express* saw an opportunity for Salvation Army emergency aid when the Duchess of York, daughter-in-law of the Queen, was alleged by the newspapers to have a £1 million cash crisis. Formerly Sarah Ferguson, the Duchess established her own household with soaring staffing costs when her marriage to Prince Andrew collapsed. Reproduction by courtesy of *Express Newspapers*.

"Would you tell Miss Ferguson, we came as soon as we could."

The early-day Army in Czechoslovakia caught the eye of artist R. Hocke who, though he satirized the Salvationists, was taken with their vigor and vitality. These comic postcards seem to have been part of a lengthy series, published by Socialni Sluzba in Karliné, Prague, and lithographed by SPOL at Pardubice, Bohemia. On the men's caps can be seen the Czech wording for The Salvation Army: "Armada Spasy." The Army "opened fire" in Czechoslovakia in 1919 and was expelled in 1950, to be recommenced in 1990.

This picture postcard was sent on August 13, 1905, from the Isle of Man, United Kingdom, to friends in Littletown, Lancashire. The writer asks on the card, "How would you like to be in the company of this old girl?"

Cartoonist Emmwood depicts leaders of Britain's Liberal Party as Salvationists outside a pub. This represents the Trades Union Movement, which had given a battering to Labor Party Leader Hugh Gaitskell for his advocacy of nuclear disarmament. Jeremy Thorpe holds the "Come and join us" placard. Joe Grimmond, leader of the Liberals, bangs the drum. Courtesy of the *Daily Mail.*

With Very Best wishes, Sincerely, Emmwood 19

To show that despite his cartoonist fun about the Army, he had only utmost respect for Salvationists, Emmwood sent this cartoon to headquarters, showing himself giving full salute with his paintbrush to a marching column.

Salvation Army Captain: "When the serpent tempted Eve—"
Bill: "Oh, chuck it. There warn't no bloomin' snake. He'd
on'y got to say, 'Here, my dear, be sure and don't touch them
'ere happles,' and she'd jolly soon a'cleaned the 'ole tree."

From the PHIL MAY series of postcards, printed in England in 1906
by Raphael Tuck and Sons, art publishers to their majesties, the
King and Queen. May's dig at journalists (following page)
appeared in "Phil May's Annual," 1895.

continued: "But, remember, it is Sunday—SO PLEASE SWIM SLOWLY."

During the twenty-five consecutive years that Alf voluntarily served at the National School, it became his particular duty to supervise the adjudication of the boys' playing skills on arrival and then to allocate them to the various bands, according to their merit.

Thus on the first night, assembled in the school hall, two hundred young people would await Alf's menacing tread down the center aisle from the rear of the auditorium to the stage. He always carried the same leather briefcase containing the all-important information. Making the most of every breath holding second, Alf would open the case slowly and carefully extract the papers detailing his decisions.

Over the years, the briefcase came to show signs of wear and tear. On the glorious 25th anniversary of his staff role at the school, the boys agreed to have a "whip round" and buy him a brand new case. Amidst much jubilation, they presented it to him at the welcome meal.

Came the same fateful moment. Following his customary procedure, Alf duly arrived at the assembly hall and, holding aloft his brand new briefcase, he made his way with steady tread down the center aisle—to the cheers of the boys.

Safely reaching the center stage podium, he opened his lovely new case, then fumbled inside—AND PRODUCED THE OLD FAITHFUL BRIEFCASE FROM WHICH HE SLOWLY DREW THE AUDITION RESULTS.

The cheers, applause and hilarious laughter were for a greatly loved and highly respected lover of the Lord and his children.

As though his twenty-five years of annual additional voluntary service at the music school were not enough, Bandmaster Alf Springate agreed to become Divisional Bandmaster for all corps in the Canterbury Division, as well as being responsible for his own band at Gillingham.

From his days as the Commanding Officer of Canterbury Temple, Major Clifford Kent recalls a rehearsal for small bands of the division held at Ashford, conducted by Divisional Bandmaster Springate.

Some members, attempting music of a higher standard than that which they normally played, were a little apprehensive. Alf knew what to say to calm their fears: "Ladies and gentlemen, this music is in four flats. PLAY AS MANY AS YOU CAN!"

OF ALL CHALLENGES, that of presenting a music program to a jail audience can be the toughest of all. While genuinely appreciative of The Salvation Army, the inmates sometimes have an opportunity to cheer themselves up by having a laugh at the visitors' expense.

The Lt.-Colonel accompanying one band to a prison decided to "have a few words" and allow the bandsmen to relax momentarily between items. "These men give their time without any payment, they buy their own uniforms, they contribute to the cost of their instruments and music, they are happy to use their talents in the Lord's service. You see, these are men with conviction."

"SO ARE WE," shouted a prisoner to a chorus of cheers.

As the Salvation Army chaplain at Parkhurst Prison, the now Reverend John Mowat took along a party of university students to assist in the chapel service. They formed themselves into an instrumental ensemble. The bass trombone player gave a talk and used his instrument as an illustration.

Moving the slide up and down, he explained, "You see, this slide goes in and out." Before he could continue, a prisoner leapt up and quipped, "That's just like us, mister."

When Coventry Stoke Band visited Shrewsbury prison, the bandmaster carefully checked the program. He wanted no faux pas on such a sensitive occasion. A professional gentleman, who did much good work in the prison voluntarily, was invited to be chairman. He did well until toward the end of the program he glanced at his watch and declared, "My word! Doesn't time fly in here."

Stories abound of such little slips, enough to make one wonder if they were all unintentional. Colonel George Fuller, famous Bandmaster of the International Staff Band from 1923 to 1942, is credited with having attempted to get a prison audience to sing along with the band.

He outlined the words of a chorus and added, "Come along now, you can easily learn those words. You're good at picking things up."

It surely must have been an error when one famous band decided to open its jail program with the stirring festival march, "Fling Wide the Gates."

When the Canadian Staff Band was invited to perform for inmates in the maximum security prison in Pittsburgh, Pennsylvania, there was tension in the air. Each bandsman had to sign in. They were ushered through two sets of iron security doors in small groups. The walls and ceiling of the auditorium were black with the soot of fires started in a riot the week before.

The voluntary audience was small when the concert commenced. Slowly more began to gather. Then cornet soloist Deryck Diffey began to glissando his way through the jazz intricacies of "Negro Spirituals." A crowd hurried in. Excitement mounted. Inmates literally began to stand on their seats for a better view of this skilled musician. The applause as Deryck concluded was deafening and demands for an encore could not be denied. Another riot was not a good idea.

Once again, Deryck performed. A front-row gentleman was almost beside himself with delight. "Man," he yelled, "we need you in here to play in our band."

"WHAT DO I HAVE TO DO TO GET IN?" Deryck called back.

THE OCCASIONS WHEN BAND and songster brigades are invited to take their music and evangelism to another Salvation Army corps are always eagerly anticipated. Rehearsal is intensified. For the host corps organizer, the work of publicizing the visit and attracting sizable congregations is no small matter—nor is that of finding families willing to billet free of charge the visiting musicians, usually in pairs. A really good night's sleep and adequate food can make a big difference to a weekend visit.

But the willingness of Salvationists and non-Salvationists alike to host visiting comrades is phenomenal. Indeed, some folk will be quite hurt if not asked to accommodate the visitors, for lasting friendships are made. Even marriages have resulted from such "specialing" weekends, to quote one of the Army's most familiar pieces of jargon.

As an example of extremely generous hosting, the experience of Bandsmen Sven Erik Ljungholm and Bob Getz takes some beating. As members of the Chicago Staff Band, they were visiting Peoria, Illinois, in 1961. The Saturday evening festival attracted a packed out crowd and afterwards they looked in vain for their hosts. However, they had been given their name and address so they set out on their own to find the home of these kind people who were to look after them.

Even in the twilight they had no difficulty in locating the attractive house listed on their billeting slip. "We are the two Salvation Army bandsmen you have agreed to look after," they cheerily announced when a charming lady answered the door.

"Do come in," she responded "How nice to meet you! Make yourselves comfortable in here," she said directing them into her lounge. "Coffee and sandwiches okay?"

It was only during conversation while eating with her, when they apologized for not meeting her after the festival, that the truth emerged. SHE WAS NOT THEIR HOST. SHE KNEW NOTHING ABOUT THE BAND'S VISIT.

~~~

THE GREAT MAJORITY OF BILLETS are ideal. But occasionally a visiting musician finds a situation not quite to his liking. A Hanwell bandsman was embarrassed by his host's dog constantly jumping up on his lap while he tried to eat his Sunday lunch.

"Oh, take no notice," said the well-meaning lady of the house, "it's just because you've got his plate."

Colonel Joseph Beaumont and Lt.-Colonel Harold Read were two of the most carefully groomed, sartorially elegant and well-spoken officers in the International Staff Band. They were personal friends and always billeted together. During long distance coach journeys, they would produce the most succulent looking sandwiches and, with pristine white servi-ettes across their knees, eat with a refinement that left other lesser mortals feeling unworthy to associate with them.

When the band arrived at a small industrial town in the north of England, it became quickly evident that the local organizer had found difficulty in securing enough billets. "I hope they'll be all right," he announced to the staff bands-men. "Not all your hosts are Salvationists, but I'm sure they'll make you feel at home." It was a brave attempt at reassurance.

Joseph and Harold took the cards bearing their host's name and address and placed them carefully in the inside pockets of their immaculate uniforms. After the commence-ment festival, they made their way along the narrow road of terraced houses to their desired haven and knocked on the door. Brushing back her hair and trying to untie her apron strings at the same time, a motherly soul opened the door.

" 'ello, lads," she cried. "I asked for two rough and ready ones so I know exactly the sort of lads you are. Come on in. Make thee sels at 'ome."

Not surprisingly, Joseph and Harold were known by their fellow bandsmen for quite a time as "Rough" and "Ready."

≈

THE MUSICIAN (the greatly lamented former weekly periodical for Army music-makers), in its issue for December 31, 1955, recorded a kind of discouragement that not often confronts a "specialing" organizer. While busily promoting the visit of the International Staff Band to Ipswich Citadel, Bandsman Woodhouse called on a retired octogenarian. "Do come and hear the band," pleaded organizer Woodhouse.

"I've no need," replied the veteran. "I've already heard them. It must have been in 1895." He then proceeded to recall the program items played, all of sixty years before. "Mind you," he concluded, "I expect that some of the men will no longer be in the band."

~~

CONSIDERING THE NUMBER OF JOURNEYS under-taken by Salvation Army bands and songster brigades, it is cause for thankfulness that the occasions when mishaps occur—or even when groups arrive late—are rare. Increasingly, they travel not only within their own lands, but some top-line sections receive invitations from overseas.

As retired Commissioner Edward Carey, of the USA, points out, the day has long gone when Army music stan-dards were well represented by the story of the man who inquired of his friend what The Salvation Army was.

"Oh," came the reply, "they're the people who stand on the street corner telling you where you will go if you don't behave yourself. Then the band plays and gives you a sample of what it will be like."

The Movement has been well served by such skilled musi-cians as those who have been members of its International Music Editorial Department. One head of that department, Colonel Albert Jakeway, was heard to tell how he received a parcel of manuscript music from a would-be composer over-seas. It was marked, "Music Manuscript - No commercial value." "A totally accurate description," quipped the Colonel.

He may have been the same music department head who, as Eric Ball related, received another parcel of compositions from an eager writer, together with a letter reading, "I am sending you this just as God gave it to me."

Back went the ms, together with a letter saying, "Thank you, dear friend, for allowing us to see your manuscript. We are now returning it, just as God gave it to you."

BUT BACK TO THE RIGORS of the journeys undertaken by our music sections.

The Cambridge Heath Band and Songster Brigade were returning to London, wearily but triumphantly from a successful Saturday evening music festival shared with Bristol Easton Road Band in Bristol's famous Colston Hall. No speedy motorway linked Bristol with London in those days. The route lay across Wiltshire along the narrow, winding A4 road.

A late-night return was inevitable, no small matter since the following morning at 10 a.m. the bandsmen and songsters would be expected to begin a full Sunday's service at the "Heath." Most were trying to take a cat-nap on the swaying coach, when one of the older ladies called out, "I don't feel well. Can we stop the coach?"

Knowing what further delay would mean for the travelers, it was suggested that they should open the coach door and have the dear soul stand in the rushing fresh air. She did so, breathing deeply. A minute later she cried out again, this time her pronunciation less distinct.

"Af loft ma teeth," she screamed.

"Pull in, driver," commanded Deputy Songster Leader Gordon Jewkes. It might be a fruitless quest, but duty demanded he should make the effort. Back along the A4 he trotted, head bent low as he peered at the ground in the darkness for the missing denture.

On the coach the bandsmen and songsters were sympathetic, but wearily they muttered to each other about the hopelessness of the search. "He'll never find them…waste of time trying…let's club together and buy her a new set…"

The minutes ticked by. Then the midnight silence was broken by a footfall on the coach steps, the sliding door being slammed and the sonorous voice of the ever-cool Gordon Jewkes speaking in the matter-of-fact tones of a man who made a habit of achieving miracles.

"Carry on, driver. I've found the missing teeth."

With hindsight, one can see this was the kind of success one would expect of a man destined to become Governor of the Falkland Islands, end his career as British Consul General in New York and be knighted by HM the Queen. Well done, Sir Gordon!

—

THE MANPOWER REPRESENTED by the average-sized Salvation Army band is considerable and is often called on for all sorts of tasks. The band at Leigh-on-Sea Corps, Essex, UK, abruptly ended its weekly rehearsal when the Commanding Officer (Major John Dale) dashed into the hall to announce that his son Paul, with his pal, had been missing for some hours in the fog which had blacked-out much of that mouth-of-the-river area. The bandsmen at once volunteered to assist the police and police dog Rikki in the search.

For two hours, they combed the scrub covered slopes of Hadleigh Downs. Dense fog made the flashlights carried by the searchers almost useless. "Let's go and get our instruments," someone suggested.

Lying huddled together for warmth under a bush near to the foot of the old Hadleigh Castle, the two boys heard the familiar sounds of the band and began to shout for help until they were located. By the playing of "All's Well" on a cornet, the other searchers were informed that the lads had been located.

Paul Dale later told how, having a day off from school, he and his pal had gone on the slopes to play. The fog came down so suddenly, they just couldn't see where they were going.

A bandsman of a neighboring corps cryptically commented: "Leigh-on-Sea Band was ideal for the job—the best fortissimo players in the land."

—

THOUGH A SALVATION ARMY OFFICER will try to give

equal care to all the flock, it is a wise officer who recognizes that the invariably attentive and usually witty bandsmen should be a special interest group in the congregation. Commissioner David A. Baxendale recalls that when he and his wife commanded their second corps, Paterson, New Jersey, his large band and songster brigade were indeed a blessing, but the bandsmen could at times be a little boisterous.

One Sunday morning, inspiration seemed to lend him wings and he found himself speaking unusually eloquently. Rather blithely he said, "I was in the washroom this morning, thinking about this message, when I cut my face shaving."

Clearly audible from the cornet section came the stage whisper: "He should have been thinking about his shaving and cut the message!"

Corps officers, when conducting a service, often have trouble "signaling" to the Bandmaster when they want to say something between the verses of a hymn, or else have the congregation sing on each verse without interruption.

Captain Beverly Ivany recalls from her teenage days that her father became frustrated each Sunday at a large corps in British Columbia, Canada. Because the bandsmen were located on the platform directly behind the songsters, who were directly behind the officer, it was extremely difficult for the bandmaster to see the subtle hand signals made by her father; or to see his slight movement toward the mike when he wanted to say an appropriate word.

A brilliant idea came to mind. Her dear dad worked on it all week. With wires extending under the carpet from podium to the bandmaster's music stand, he set up a "red-light, green-light" system. He took Bev to the citadel on the Saturday to make sure everything was in order. When he wanted the singing to continue, the "green-light" told the bandmaster to keep waving the baton. The "red-light" bade him hush the music when words of wisdom were needed.

At 10:30 a.m. on the first Sunday of the invention, a certain cornet player caught wind of what was to happen. He switched the wires. At 11 a.m. the opening, triumphant song was a disaster. Father pushed the green button. Total silence. After the next verse, father pushed the red button. He did his best to speak over the playing of the band. Poor dad! He should have known that bandsmen will be bandsmen, says Bev!

~~~

IT IS OFTEN AT THE END of a tiring Sunday that a sudden impishness will strike a group of bandsmen. There are two approaches to the Army citadel at Hendon, North London. One is through a narrow alleyway between other buildings, handy for individual members of the congregation hurrying along to be in time for the service. The other is by the actual road which is a turning from off the main road, and of course a longer approach to the hall.

One hot Sunday evening, the excellent Hendon Citadel Band was marching with customary precision from its 6 p.m. open-air meeting. Having several members of Her Majesty's guards bands as Salvationists also inevitably added to the band's marching skills. The day had begun at 10 a.m., with afternoon duties as well. Now only the evening meeting remained.

Normally, the music chosen for the march would take the band round from the main street into the side street and be triumphantly completed outside the hall. But not tonight. The drummer's two double-taps ended the march just as the flag sergeants and the corps officers had passed the alleyway on the left. Then the front row of trombones reached the alleyway.

On sudden uncontrollable impulse, the trombonist on the inside left nearest the alleyway shouted, "LEFT TURN." As to a man, the entire front row "left turned" and marched smartly up the alleyway. Each succeeding row did likewise, giggling like naughty schoolboys as they hustled into their bandroom.

Meanwhile two flag sergeants and the Major and his wife marched blissfully onward up the main street, unaware that their flanks were bare.

It is as well to know that bandsmen will be bandsmen.

CHAPTER 5

AS IT HATH PLEASED ALMIGHTY GOD

OPPOSITES ARE SURPRISINGLY CLOSE TOGETHER. Laughter and tears; sorrow and merriment; solemnity and hilarity have only the finest line drawn between them, as most Salvation Army officers early learn when they commence their ministry to needy humanity.

No situation demands more understanding from a minister and more genuine compassion for the family involved than the final illness and death of a loved one. And no ceremony requires more competent and thoughtful handling by an officer than a funeral service. Yet, even on such a significant occasion, no amount of forethought can exclude the possibility of a totally unexpected incident threatening to undermine the gravity and turn the serious into the comical.

Captain Beverly Ivany recalls that when she and husband David were appointed to one corps, within a short time a prominent personality there was promoted to Glory. The day of the funeral service was set. Rather than try to find a baby-sitter for her three- and five-year old children, Bev decided it would be a good "life experience" for them both to attend. She has always been very avant garde and progressive in the upbringing of her four delightfully precocious children.

Five-year-old Kirsten had attended two other funeral services. But little Joshua had been to only one before, that of Bev's Uncle Stan, six months previously. At that time, she and David had tried to explain as much as a little boy could handle.

The funeral service was about to begin. She said to the two children: "Now, remember, people here are very sad. We must keep quiet and sit still. It won't take a long time."

The band played the prelude. Everyone turned to see Captain David Ivany proceeding down the center aisle. Following him were the pallbearers, then the casket. Everyone was still. Not a sound was heard. When...suddenly...little Joshua yelled out,

"WELL, HERE COMES UNCLE STAN AGAIN!"

On arriving in Johannesburg City, South Africa, having been appointed there from Cape Town after several years' service in the UK, Captain and Mrs. George Stoner were eager to learn about their new responsibilities in a totally new situation as quickly as possible. The comprehensive "brief" left by the previous corps officer warned George that one aged member of his flock was dying and as the new Commanding Officer he would want to introduce himself to the family without delay.

George hurried over to pray with the departing Salvationist and to learn from his family their plans for the funeral services, which were certain to be only a few days away. It had already been agreed with George's predecessor that there would be a service of tribute at the Army hall, followed immediately by the committal service at the graveside.

The new Captain handled the Citadel service well. Then, in his own car, he followed the funeral cortege, determined to keep close to the last funeral car, for he had no idea in a large city totally new to him where the cemetery was situated.

Crossroads were ahead, controlled by traffic lights. To George's dismay they changed to "stop" as the last limousine crossed over. It seemed an age before the green light showed again. George sped over. Where was the cortege? Oh, what relief, there were the black cars! He fell in behind again.

The cars parked at the cemetery gates. As a mark of respect, the mourners would process on foot to the graveside. George took his place at the head of them, to be greeted by a clergyman in pastoral collar and suit. "Hello, Captain," he said cordially, "and what are you doing?"

"The lot," said George, in expansive, somewhat back-slapping style, relieved that the first service had gone so smoothly and that he had caught up again with the family mourners. The clergyman smiled happily.

Arriving at the open graveside, George allowed just a moment for the mourners to gather round, then he stepped forward and began to read from Scripture. "The Lord is my Shepherd, I shall not want," he declared, and felt himself warming in sympathy and support toward the grieving family.

"Yea, though I walk through the valley of the shadow of death…" George faltered momentarily. A doubt had crossed his mind even as he read on. He was new, of course, but he couldn't really remember having seen before any of the dear folk clustered around him. Out of the corner of his eye, he suddenly saw one of his own uniformed bandsmen at the edge of an adjoining field, waving, waving…

"…and I will dwell in the house of the Lord for ever. AMEN," he intoned in hurried finality. "God bless you all!" With a sudden close of his Bible, George leapt away to join his own mourning flock.

He has often since wondered what the unknown pastor thought of this unexpected takeover by the Salvation Army man.

Of all experiences confronting a newly commissioned officer, that of conducting the first funeral service is surely the most onerous of all. During cadet training days, procedures are explained and the Army's "Book of Ceremonies" is reasonably explicit, but only actual experience can really teach.

Soon after arriving at his first appointment, a brand new Lieutenant from the USA Western Territory's School for Officer Training received a telephone call from a man explaining that his wife had died. She had been a junior soldier in the Army as a child and, although having not attended for many years, had always regarded herself as a Salvationist. He knew she would want to be buried under the Army colors.

The Lieutenant agreed. He was impressed that they had been married for thirty-nine years. Was there a particular song the husband would like to have sung during the service? Yes, indeed there was. No, it wasn't a hymn, but he had it on tape and would arrange for it to be played at the service.

Introducing the unknown tape recording, the fledgling officer invited the congregation to reflect on the thirty-nine years' bliss which the departed had shared with her husband. What an example this was in an age when so many took the marriage vow so lightly! He urged his listeners to reflect prayerfully on their own family life as they listened to the tape.

The recorder was switched on. Loudly and clearly came the voice of Jim Reeves: "Please release me, let me go, for I don't love you anymore."

~~

Brigadier John Thompson confirms that one's first funeral service experience can be nerve-racking. He remembers the experience of another Lieutenant who, when conducting a cremation service, accidentally touched too soon the button on the podium which automatically slowly lowers the casket out of sight or closes curtains in front of it. "Come back," said the lad officer in desperation, "I haven't finished yet."

The Brigadier also recalls the cremation service he conducted for a fine Salvationist in Leeds. He had advised the color sergeant to stand to one side of the coffin, but that worthy rather dogmatically asserted his place was at the foot of the casket facing the congregation. When the curtains closed, and the color sergeant also went out of sight, the Brigadier refrained from actually saying, "I told you so."

After escorting the mourners from the chapel, Brigadier Thompson returned to see what had happened to his color sergeant. He found him struggling to unmesh the chromium top of the flag from the crematorium curtain rings. Finally, in his obdurate way, he gave the flagpole a tug and pulled the curtain down over himself.

Somewhat tongue-in-cheek, the relatives requested that the following Sunday's moments-of-tribute include the chorus, "We'll never let the old flag fall."

Brigadier Thompson's one other funeral memory is of an aged retired officer who was so eager to get to heaven, he planned his funeral services personally well in advance, insisting on vibrant, vigorous songs. He also requested the funeral director not to line his casket with any kind of nylon because his skin was sensitive to it and instructed his daughter to limit the flowers accepted because of his hay fever allergies.

~

Will you mind who conducts your funeral service? There is a great deal of evidence to show that many people are very choosy indeed about the officiating minister and go to considerable lengths to get the person of their choice—as this recollection of Major Arthur J. Brown makes plain:

When Maureen wrote to us asking that we call upon her the next time we were in Holyhead, she described her reason as "important but not urgent." Maureen had been one of our junior soldiers almost thirty years previously when we had commanded the former corps at Holyhead, and her mother had been one of our soldiers.

"Important but not urgent?" I queried with my wife.

"She probably wants to discuss her mother's funeral," answered Audrey.

"But Elsie is not dead," I protested.

"No difference," shrugged Audrey, "it's the funeral."

In due course we presented ourselves at Maureen's home. Besides my wife, there was the little trio of Elsie, in the best of health, who spoke little English; Maureen who was fluently bilingual; and myself, who had enough Welsh to follow the conversation between mother and daughter.

Said Maureen: "It's my mother's funeral. I want you to promise that you will do it for me." (My wife gave me her "Told you so" smile.)

"Yes, of course," I responded at once. There seemed little else that I could say.

As the conversation proceeded, Elsie would interrupt every so often and ask, in Welsh, what we were talking about.

"Nothing to do with you, mother," Maureen would answer, in Welsh, of course. "Mind your own business!"

And so, in the presence of the un-deceased, we planned, sealed and settled the whole arrangements. Strangely enough, I conducted Elsie's funeral service within the year!

As we came away from the graveside, another former Holyhead Salvationist, Mrs. Ecc we called her, quickened her step to walk by my side.

"A lovely funeral, Major, a lovely funeral. I wonder, Major, WOULD YOU DO MINE FOR ME?"

~

Finally, let it be said again, that when it comes to conducting funeral services, nothing must be unplanned, nothing left to chance—as Captain John Moore, of Canada, would now be the first to agree:

I've conducted more funeral services than any of my cadet training session mates. In fact, I think I've done more funerals than all of them combined. It seems to go that way, doesn't it? Bruce Power is way ahead of the rest of us in infant dedications, and James Hardman is the leader in performing marriage ceremonies. Me? I bury 'em.

So, you'd think I would have known better when the

grieving widow at my most recent funeral asked me, prior to the ceremony, if she might be permitted to sing a solo during the service.

I know, I know. I should have known better. The very least I should have done was to have asked what she intended to sing. But it had been one of those weeks in which officers tend to get a wee bit distracted and I just let it go. "She'll likely sing one of his favorite hymns," I thought.

I knew something was amiss after I had introduced her to the large number of friends who had gathered behind her at the podium. She grabbed the microphone from its stand and, Las Vegas-style, flipped the long mike-cord behind her as she walked slowly, dramatically toward her late dearly beloved reposed in his casket.

She pointed her finger at the organist (with whom she had obviously prearranged things) in one of those "Hit-it-baby!" gestures. An arpeggio swept from the organist...

And the widow, cradling the microphone and gazing dreamily at the face of her dead husband, softly crooned,

"STAY AS SWEET AS YOU ARE..."

CHAPTER 6

THERE'S A WAY
OF SAYING THINGS

T HERE'S NO DENYING THAT SALVATIONISTS do a lot
  of talking—public talking, that is. They are exhorted to
"preach the word," to be able and willing "to give.... a reason
of the hope that is in (them)." Soon after transferring from
the young people's band to the senior band in their mid-teens,
a young fellow or woman will find his or her name listed to
conduct a Sunday morning open-air meeting and, if they
haven't previously studied how one goes about such a task,
their mind will be wonderfully concentrated now. What does
a meeting leader do and say?

Sunday school, Bible studies, corps cadet classes, youth
groups, and so much more, make the average Salvationist
well aware that this militant brand of Christianity commits
them to developing an excellence in communication. There
is, after all, a way of saying things. What follows is a small
collection of the apposite word.

A recently converted man was giving his testimony in Australian Congress meetings being conducted by General and Mrs. Wilfred Kitching. He did not, as do some converts, dwell at all upon his misdeeds (possibly to the disappointment of some in the audience). Instead he simply declared, "God has buried my sins in the deepest sea, and he has put up a notice: 'NO FISHING!'"

As newly appointed British Commissioner, Denis Hunter was being welcomed during a mid-week meeting at a small Norfolk corps. The local Corps Sergeant-Major, a man with a fine broad accent, had been deputed to give the oration. "Arrrh, Oi must say Oi loikes the look of this man," he began. "Oi don't knows 'im, but Oi loikes the look of 'im. 'E's got what Oi call a tea-pot face, noice and round-like. Not what Oi calls a coffee-pot face, all long and narrer. 'E's gonna be orl roight, 'e is."

"I love The Salvation Army. So did my father. They used to bring him home every Saturday night."
—*Bob Hope, speaking during a U.S.A. Western Territory centennial festival held in the Dorothy Chandler Auditorium, Los Angeles, 1980.*

Seen on a poster outside a Salvation Army citadel in Stockport, England: "JESUS THE CARPENTER NEEDS JOINERS. APPLY HERE ANY SUNDAY." (Reported in *Reader's Digest*, October 1989.) A passerby congratulated the Commanding Officer on hammering home the message.

～～

When as a young man the brilliant Scandinavian American composer Erik Leidzen worked for Colonel Povlsen, he asked him, "Is it true, Colonel, that you can speak in seven languages?" His fellow-Scandinavian replied, "Yes, I can speak seven languages, but I can keep my mouth shut in all seven." (*Sagas of Salvationism*, Wm. G. Harris.)

～～

During meetings marking his retirement from active officership and as National Commander of all Salvation Army service in the United States, Commissioner Holland French revealed he had acquired the name "Holland" because his father (a notable officer himself) had so thoroughly enjoyed the years he had spent when appointed to that country. Quipped the Commissioner, "I am just so thankful he never served in Mesopotamia."

～～

For cadets studying at the International Training College, London, an emotional, intellectual and spiritual highlight of the curriculum is the monthly Spiritual Day, so called because for a full day the essential qualities that go to make a successful Salvation Army officer are under close review.

On a day in 1946, the awe-inspiring principle speaker was General Albert Orsborn, acknowledged since as the last of the Army's truly great orator-Generals. Among those sharing the platform was Colonel Emma Davies, an unmarried woman officer with outstanding personality and who carried chief responsibility for the training of the women cadets. The Colonel was invited to lead the cadets and congregation in the old Charles Wesley hymn, "Surrounded by a host of foes, Stormed by a host of foes within." To encourage the large company to sing as she felt the hymn should be sung, she outlined in dramatic tones the full first verse.

As she read, "Single, yet undismayed, I am," she sensed a smile on the face of the General beside her, he seeing an application to her singleness not intended by Wesley. Drawing herself to her full not inconsiderable height, the spinster Colonel pointed to the colonel trimmings on her upright collar and laughingly but proudly declared, "No man put these badges on my shoulder, General."

〜

Commandant Lovett, of Philadelphia, sought to be as patient as she could with an alcoholic who, time after time, stepped forward to kneel at the Penitent-form and claim God's help to be free from his addiction. But he seemed to be the compulsive backslider. On one occasion, as she knelt beside him and heard him yet again profess victory, she exclaimed, "Dear Lord, take him home now while he's still saved!"

〜

"We used to have a retired Colonel in our corps at Caterham who would often say when speaking during open-air meetings, 'Some people say there is no such place as hell, but when they are annoyed they tell you to go there'."

〜

Commissioner Alexander M. Damon sometimes posed the question during youth councils in the USA, "What is the difference between a youth chewing gum and a cow chewing the cud?"

Answer: "The thoughtful expression on the cow's face."

〜

Colonel Reginald Bovan had a distinguished career as a Salvation Army officer. The three aspects of it which interested him most of all were the years he spent as drummer with the International Staff Band, the time he was the executive secretary of the Army's famous Mothers' Hospital at Clapton, London, and his final appointment as Chief

Secretary of the Men's Social Services, dealing principally with needy men. When giving his life-story, he would begin: "My career can be summed up in three words—drums, mums and bums."

Major John Fairbank was noted for his ability to see the best in people. In some exasperation with his saintliness, one day his daughter Ruth (later Mrs. Commissioner Geoffrey Dalziel) said to him, "Father, you'd see good even in the devil."

"Well," replied her dad, "you must admit he's a hard worker, isn't he!"

A group of St. Albans bandsmen stood looking from the Army citadel door at the swirling snow, wondering if it would ease in time for them to conduct their regular Sunday morning open air meeting. Without saying a word, Bandsman Alan Dockree stepped out into the snowflakes, raised his trombone to his lips and blew a single note. "What was that for?" asked his astonished colleagues. "That," replied Alan, "was C amidst the winter's snow."

Arriving at the Army's Sunbury-on-Thames Conference Centre, delegates to a territorial corps cadet house party found they were divided into groups under named discussion group leaders. Within minutes, an enthusiastic corps cadet thought she had located her leader. "Are you Iris Port?" she asked. "No, I'm Olive Bottle," came the stunning reply. A warm spirit prevailed throughout the week.

—*Iris Port*

In the subdued light of some public house and club bars, it is often difficult for customers to distinguish the value of coins they are giving in the Army collecting box when purchasing

The War Cry. "Must make sure that it's not a 50-pence piece," said one young man. To which his neighbor retorted, "Didn't you know that if you put a 50-pence piece in his box, his cap band lights up!"

—*Charles Prodgers*

The Colonel, with his wife, was visiting his secretary's mother in the hospital. This retired Salvation Army officer, so vigorous and effective in her active service days, was now becoming quite forgetful. The Colonel inquired how she was. "I am so glad," she replied in what had become quite a deep voice...then faltering a little, she began again, "I am so glad..." Once more she tried, "I am so glad..." Turning to her daughter, she asked, "Ruth, dear, what have I got to be glad about?"

—*Ruth Reeve*

It was our first corps command after having been commissioned as Salvation Army officers. The members of our flock were generous to a fault as I visited and prayed with them. Before I left their homes almost invariably they would say, "Take these cookies (or cake or pie) to Mrs. Baxendale. I have made them just for both of you." Knowing the high price of the ingredients and the work in preparation, I tried to be reluctant, but they kept insisting.

I thought I would try another tactic. When one kind comrade offered me a beautiful lemon pie, I said, "I insist I help pay for this. Let me give you a dollar." (It was almost forty years ago!) I reached into my pocket and, horror of horrors, I found I had only ninety cents.

Quite undismayed, my soldier said, "Oh, Lieutenant, I'll take the rest out in your Sunday sermon."

With sudden boldness I responded, "But I don't have any ten cent sermons!"

"Well, Lieutenant," she answered, "I'll come twice!"

—*David Baxendale*

For the young Lieutenant stationed at a south coast corps in Britain, the simmering antagonism between his songster leader and one of his bandsmen was a cause of deep distress. Faithfully, he spoke to each one privately about how dishonoring to God and the Army such barely concealed feelings were. They must end their bickering if the corps and God's Kingdom were to be built. Grudgingly, the two resolved to try to do better.

But one hot Sunday afternoon, just before the open-air meeting on a crowded beach was to begin, the two rivals got into an argument. Losing his temper, the bandsman struck the songster leader, who promptly hit back. Within a moment, they were rolling in their uniforms on the sand while the frantic Lieutenant did his best to calm them.

A crowd gathered quickly. The two were separated. The open air meeting was canceled. The Lieutenant remained, holding the promenade rail, gazing heartbroken out to sea.

A bystander put his hand encouragingly on the officer's arm and offered sympathy. It was just the kind word the Lieutenant needed to pour out his heart and the whole story to the stranger. Little did he know that the kind counselor was a local "stringer" for the national newspapers.

Next morning, a Monday when the media is usually short of copy, the country's main newspapers told the holiday-resort story of Salvation Army fisticuffs. Top marks for punchy skill had to go to the headline writer who was aware of some of William Booth's historic utterances. His headline was: "WHY SHOULD THE DEVIL HAVE ALL THE BEST FIGHTS?"

Guest speaker Captain Chick Yuill from Britain was being introduced by Major Tom Jones at the USA Southern Territory's famed Bible Conference. The Major not only wanted the Captain to feel very welcome, but also wanted the congregation to realize the excellence of their guest as speaker, writer, original thinker and organizer. Indeed, in no department of life did Captain Yuill fall short.

With much modesty the Scotsman responded to his effusive welcome. "Why," he said, "if I were only half that good, I would have been elected General." The Army's 1986 High Council had just elected General Eva Burrows.

Southern Territorial Commander Commissioner Andrew S. Miller (who had accepted nomination for generalship at that High Council) leapt to his feet. "I am half as good, but they didn't elect me," he lamented.

~

Colonel Eva Burrows, later to become only the second woman General of The Salvation Army, was being welcomed and installed as Territorial Commander for Sri Lanka by General Arnold Brown. "Tradition has it," began General Brown, "that when they were expelled from the Garden of Eden, Adam and Eve set out to make Sri Lanka their home. Well, you can see that Eve has made it, but what happened to Adam?

—*Lyell Rader, Lt.- Colonel (R), D.D., O.F., as told him by* The War Cry *editor Lyell Rader, Jr.*

~

Adjutant Albert Moss's special pleasure when conducting meetings was to take with him those who had known the transforming power of God as he had done. One such was giving his testimony and, after the manner of such trophies, was enlarging on the twenty years he had served the devil.

Around the open-air meeting were men of a Yorkshire regiment, then stationed in the Cape. To these the trophy repeated, "Twenty years, twenty years I served him."

"Eh, lad," called out a wag, "if tha'd served another year, tha'd gotten a pension!"

—*from* Well Played *by General Frederick Coutts.*

CHAPTER 7

THEY, TOO, ARE GOD'S CHILDREN

DALE CARNEGIE'S CLASSIC, *How to Win Friends and Influence People*, makes twelve promises even before its preface. The ninth pledge assures readers that it will "help you to handle complaints, avoid arguments, keep your human contacts smooth and pleasant."

If Mr. Carnegie's book can fulfill its promises, then the newly commissioned Salvation Army officer would do well to keep it accessible on a bookshelf alongside the Bible, Song Book, Handbook of Doctrine and Orders and Regulations for Officers. Dealing with people will almost certainly be the biggest challenge to be faced during the succeeding thirty, forty years.

Just as people come in all shapes and sizes, so do they come in degrees of kindness, thoughtfulness, cheerfulness, generosity, saintliness, common sense, attractiveness, even cleanliness. And the devoted Army officer must seek to love them all, minister to them all, and lead them upward toward what the hymn-writer calls "the holy hill of God." For they are all God's children.

To quote the famous Mr. Carnegie again, "The craving in everyone is to be appreciated." Some labor long without achieving that goal. Fresh from the School for Officer Training, 22-year-old Lieutenant Henry Arrowood wondered how the congregation at Greenwood, South Carolina, would receive him as their new Commanding Officer. His predecessor had been aged 58. Would a mere Lieutenant be regarded as just a rookie, an innocent abroad?

He was warmly welcomed, but amid the many kind words spoken, the comment of a 75-year-old man, rejoicing in the name of Augustus Quattlebaum, stayed with him. "This corps has had its ups and downs through the years," said Augustus, stretching out his hand in welcome, "but it hasn't been the same since E.P. Steadham was stationed here."

Henry's two-year term at the corps sped by swiftly and successfully. After his final farewell meeting, he was alone in the office, gathering up his last-minute personal desk items to take with him to his next assignment. He couldn't help overhearing and enjoying the conversation of some of his flock outside his door about his term of command: "He's done well." "We shall miss him." "I've enjoyed his preaching," etc.

Then came the familiar sound of Augustus Quattlebaum's voice: *"That may be as may be, but things ain't been the same since E.P. Steadham was stationed here."*

Not even experienced Salvation Army leaders can always command the affection they would like to receive. As a Divisional Commander, James Osborne (later to become a Commissioner and the USA National Commander) had reason to write a letter of rebuke and guidance to a corps officer. Jim and his wife Ruth were due to visit the officer's corps and conduct meetings the weekend following the dispatch of the chastening letter. But by reply came word from the unrepentant C.O.: "This letter is to uninvite you to my corps."

⌁

BY CONTRAST, THE OVER-ZEALOUS AFFECTION and kindness of some people can be a problem for officers. As a young Lieutenant, serving in the UK, Stanley Richardson would visit an old lady living near the quarters several times a week . No one else did, and he was afraid that something might happen to her, for she lived alone.

He was offered a cup of tea on each visit. The teapot was always on the hob of a very old and dirty kitchen range. The table cloth was a newspaper, the milk bottle served as a jug, and the butter stayed within its open wrapper on the table. To say the room was dirty was the understatement of the year, but the old lady regularly refused all offers of help.

Stan always managed to find a good reason for refusing her kind offer of a drink, but one day he arrived just as she had made a fresh pot of tea. He capitulated! He clenched his teeth and looked steadfastly out of the window while she poured some tea into her only chipped mug. She swilled it round and round, then with a practiced turn of the wrist, threw the contents to the back of the open fire-grate. Then she filled the mug to the brim.

As surreptitiously as possible, Lieutenant Richardson turned the mug round, picking it up with his unaccustomed left hand in the hope that the left-hand side would be less lethal than the right-hand side. Screwing up his courage he began to drink the noxious brew. As he swallowed the last mouthful, the lady looked at him with affection gleaming in her eyes.

"Eh, that's funny, Lieutenant. You are left-handed too, just like me!"

A somewhat similar experience befell Captain and Mrs. James Watt when they were stationed at Crookston, Minnesota, in the USA. A mother who had several children liked the Army officers to call on her. She was a generous lady, but not particularly clean. She was always eager for the Watts to take a meal with her family. They successfully managed to avoid that trauma until one particular day.

The telephone rang in the quarters. "Please come right away." It was Ruth, the generous mother. Dutifully, the Watts hurried round right away, wondering about the reason for the

71

urgent call. They were met at the door by a smiling Ruth. "Now I have you here and dinner is all ready for you."

There was no escaping the ordeal. Ruth instructed her oldest daughter to remove the hard-boiled eggs from the boiling water, then make the tea with the *same water.* That was one night when the Watts decided they were not thirsty, thank you very much!

~

RESPECT AND REGARD FOR OFFICERS by members of their flock will often ripen into a personal friendship that continues long after their pastor has gone to other flocks. The same Stanley Richardson recalls that his officer-parents kept in touch with old 'Uncle Bill,' as he was known, for many years.

One day, an urgent message arrived to say that the old Envoy was very ill and had been asking for "The Major." Stan's dad caught the train to his former command and spent several hours at the bedside of his sick friend. Finally, as he was about to leave, Uncle Bill took hold of his arm. "I know I am dying. Would you take this watch and chain as a memento of our friendship? It doesn't go, but it would be worth having repaired."

Next day, Major Richardson took his new acquisition to the watchmaker. His advice was the same as Uncle Bill's. It was worth repairing.

In no time at all, the timepiece—all bright, shining and ticking—complete with chain, was looking grand against Father Richardson's indispensable red waistcoat. The family agreed it added greatly to the dignity of father's appearance. Winding it up with its tiny key became almost a religious rite. When there was any reference to time on the radio, out would come the watch. The lid would be opened with a casual press of a button; there would be a grunt of satisfaction. The family could never be sure whether father was checking his watch against Big Ben or vice versa.

Mrs. Richardson and the children were becoming accustomed to the head of the household's new dignity. But then a letter arrived. It concluded: "As you can see, I am much better now. Can I have my watch back, please? Much love. Uncle Bill."

Well, some time later Uncle Bill did go to that land where time is unimportant, and the faithful shepherd of the flock received his memento back again. Father Richardson's dignity was restored.

A SOMEWHAT WHIMSICAL SONG, POPULAR at one time with male voice quartets, begins with the line, "How many queer folk in the Army we see! Good old Army!" Relaxing in his armchair in Redcliffe, Queensland, Australia, the now retired Commissioner Alistair G. Cairns has no difficulty recalling from a lifetime of service a number of well-intentioned, very sincere folk who fully justified the song-writer's assertion. For example, he writes:

When we were stationed at Sydney Congress Hall, we had some fine old warriors. One was former Color Sergeant Harpley. This grand old chap arrived in Australia after he had retired from the British Army. He had fought under General Gordon in the Battle of Khartoum. He'd won many awards for bravery and proudly wore their medals with about three rows of ribbons on his Salvation Army uniform. After he'd retired from carrying the Sydney Congress Hall Band flag, he and Mrs. Harpley would spend the whole of each Sunday in the Congress Hall, even remaining in their seats under the platform to enjoy their lunch and evening meal.

Even when Harpley became very ill, he still attended the meetings. Sadly, Mrs. Harpley was not noticing how badly spoiled her husband's uniform was getting. It was a particular concern of my wife, Margery, that Harpley's spectacles were so dirty. They were the old-fashioned metal type with the sprung lugs which held them on to his face very tightly.

Word came that Harpley had been taken to hospital. I hurried to visit him and asked if there was anything he needed. He asked for his glasses. I drove to his home in

Ultimo, an inner city area where the terraced houses were very close, very old and very run down.

When Margery saw the glasses she was so pleased. "At last, I'll be able to do something about them." After the tea dishes were washed, in went the spectacles to receive the best scrub they had ever known. I took them to Hartley right away.

Next day I returned to visit him. He was a new man. "This is a great hospital," he enthused. "The nurses are so kind. The food is great. And they must be doing me good. *I can even see better!*"

Another of the great old warriors of Sydney Congress Hall was a widow who loved to spend most of her time in the hall, cleaning, polishing and keeping the auditorium in tip-top condition. She was so busy, she seemed to have no time to care about her own appearance. Her uniform became quite bedraggled, though Margery and others tactfully encouraged her to do better. Another problem: she had no teeth, neither her own nor dentures.

What could be done? One day it seemed the problem would solve itself. A former pugilist and drunkard was converted. For obvious reasons, we called him "Punch." Cupid seemed to offer us hope when Punch proposed to our cleaning lady. She accepted and asked me to conduct the wedding ceremony. Surely, said Margery and the other ladies of the corps, the bride-to-be will now visit the dentist! But again their courage failed them in broaching the topic with her. Instead, I was deputed to mention it during the pre-marriage counseling sessions.

As tactfully as I could I asked if she planned to visit the dentist. Her reply left me speechless. "Oh, it's no problem," she replied. "Punch has a set and when I tried his, they fitted perfectly. So they'll be fine for the wedding. We'll be quite happy."

It was a lovely wedding!

Alastair Cairns' third example of people who require tactful handling concerns a couple at the corps in Redcliffe where he lives in retirement. He writes:

∽

They wanted the Army to conduct their marriage. The husband-to-be had been divorced. The lady was a widow. Her priest was unwilling to conduct the wedding because of the man's divorce. Other churches also demurred. Finally, the Salvation Army Captain, after careful inquiry into the circumstances and with official approval, agreed.

The engaged couple were so pleased, they began to attend Army meetings. Then came Mother's Day. As the service progressed, the Captain invited all mothers over a certain age to stand. His search for the oldest mother present came to a conclusion when the bride-to-be found herself standing alone as the oldest over-eighty mother present. Everyone was surprised and delighted, for she was very sprightly and looked much younger than her now revealed years. Her cup of joy was brimful when she received a box of chocolates. Alas, the Captain's kindness undermined all the arrangements in hand.

Only one person in the congregation was not delighted: the husband-to-be. "I'm not marrying a woman who's over eighty," declared the indignant male. The wedding was called off. They drifted apart.

But there was a sequel. Not long afterward, the angry gentleman passed away. His sprightly lady friend continued as healthy and sprightly as ever!

∽

THE WORKLOAD OF ARMY OFFICERS is frequently lightened by unexpected incidents that send them on their way convulsed with laughter. When my parents were stationed in an industrial north of England town, father went to visit a lady who was in bed, ill. He sat beside her bedside and offered counsel and comfort. When he rose to pray and make his departure, he noticed a small head beside her just above the bedclothes.

"Oh, hello, my little man, are you in bed keeping your mother company?" inquired father, rather surprised.

"Eeeh, major," replied the good lady, "that's me 'usband. 'E's on night shift."

It was in the same town that my dad was summoned urgently to pray with an old man who was dying. The doctor called while father was there in the bedroom. He gave one quick look at the patient and pronounced quietly, "I think he's dead."

The old chap opened his eyes. "No I ain't, doctor, no I ain't," he called weakly.

"Hold your tongue, John," instructed his wife. "The doctor knows better than you."

~~

At the Chicago Harbor Light Corps, noted for its outstanding success in helping free men from the shackles of alcohol, the Captain in charge couldn't help but eavesdrop on a private prayer meeting. Convert Charlie, who had successfully battled through his fondness for drink and had become an ardent evangelist, was praying. He had his arm around the shoulders of "Buttercup," whose name—suggestive of the untoiling flower of the field—indicated with truth that he was not over-fond of work.

"O God," prayed Charlie, "please find Buttercup a job. You know that is what he needs. If it's only $50 a week, find him a job. If it's only $40 a week, do find him a job." From this point, Charlie prayed on a diminishing scale until he cried earnestly, "If it's only ten dollars a week, please find him a job."

Buttercup stood suddenly to his feet, brushed aside Charlie's arm with obvious annoyance, and went to the window, looking out pensively. The Captain decided it was time to break in on the scene. "Don't take it to heart, Buttercup," he advised. "Charlie meant no harm."

"OK, Cap'n, OK," replied the ten-dollar toiler. "That's OK. But if this guy had kept on praying another minute, he'd a-had me workin' for nutten."

~

The gratitude of some converts for their transformation after truly handing over their lives to God is well seen in a recollection by Mrs. Lt.-Colonel Hazel Rice. A fellow who had really been "a bad guy" was genuinely saved. Shortly after his conversion, he approached his corps officer and very earnestly said: "Captain, I'm so happy. I just feel so good. I'd really like to do something for you."

"That's great," replied the Captain. "But tell me, what would you like to do? What do you think you could do?"

Thoughtfully, the convert replied: "I really don't know, Cap'n. I've been a crook all my life." Then his face brightened into a big smile. "I know, I know what I can do. I can fix your gas meter so it won't register."

~

FEW OFFICERS DEAL IN MORE DOWN-TO-EARTH situations than do those in the UK Goodwill Centres. At the time of their early day origin they were known, very appropriately, as the "Cellar, Gutter and Garret Brigade." The name may have changed but the nature of the work at the heart of overcrowded, dingy cities has not. Yet many who live in such inner city areas have a chirpy and cheerful optimism, and a loving respect for the Army officers who offer their friendship and help.

Songwriter Brigadier Gladys M. Taylor greatly admired the Goodwill Department and frequently featured its work when she was editor of *The Deliverer,* a magazine devoted to women's interests and social service. In speaking to Rotary and other clubs about Goodwill work, she would tell of the officer who called at a tiny terraced house where a rather simple little lady was in distress because her husband had died suddenly the day before.

"Tell me how it happened." the officer asked sympathetically.

"Well, I asked him to go to our little garden and cut a cabbage. As he did so, he dropped down dead."

"Oh, what a shock for you! Whatever did you do?"

"Well, what could I do! I had to open a can of peas!"

~~

Gladys also told of the Goodwill officer who entered the home of a bereaved lady to pray with her and was invited in to the front room to see the late husband in his casket. She remarked on his fine appearance. How peaceful he looked! How sun tanned, too!

"Oh, yes," responded the widow. "His holiday did him good!"

~~

The Army's famous weekly newspaper, *The War Cry* reported the occasion when a Goodwill Department officer was called to a poor home where an aged man, notorious for maltreating his wife, had just died. The officer performed the task of helping lay him out.

For a moment or two, the wife stood in silence looking at her late husband. Then she remarked, *"Well, John Henry, you didn't believe in heaven and you didn't believe in hell. Now, here you are, all dressed up with nowhere to go!"*

~~

ACROSS THE LENGTH AND BREADTH of the mighty dominion of Canada, no province can boast a more delicious sense of humor than can the people who dwell on the rocky island of Newfoundland. Their signposts will direct you to such delightful places as Little Heart's Ease, Too Good Arm or Comfort Cove, or to Deadman's Bay if you prefer the dramatic. Where else in the world do they divide their time zone by half-an-hour? Only people with a twinkle in their eye would do that.

For scholars and lovers of words, Newfoundland books make rewarding reading. The accents of the mainly English west country and Irish ancestors of the Newfoundlanders can be heard as you read from such a book as *A Whale for the Killing* by Farley Mowat: "Niver did see such a toime for caribou. I tell ye, me son, they's thicker'n flies on a fish flake, and coming right down to the landwash to pick away at the kelp. Oh, yiss bye, they's lots o' country meat on the go."

It's a land where if you go hunting you'll need a "nunnybag"—the name for a sealskin or canvas knapsack. And they'll warn you about a "nunny-fudger"—the name they give to a person who thinks more about dinner than work, one who shirks their duty.

If you're fortunate, they may serve you a "coady duff"— boiled pudding with molasses.

Newfie jokes are, of course, renowned the world over, but only those who have not lived in or spent a deal of time on the great Rock would suggest it is the humor of simpletons. For no one enjoys Newfie jokes more than the Newfoundlanders themselves and they tell such jokes about themselves more often and with greater relish than anybody. But a word of warning: if you are a visitor from "Upalong" (the Newfoundland name for mainland Canada) or from any other land, don't try telling them a Newfie joke. For if you do, you will find the temperature has dropped by twenty degrees and suddenly it is strangely quiet.

During the nearly six years my wife and I were privileged to serve in Canada, we had for much of that time the superb support and personal help of a Newfoundland officer as ADC. Whenever we flew back to Toronto Airport from a distant and energy sapping campaign, the faithful Major Ronald Goodyear would meet us—whatever the hour—with the car but a few steps from the exit, no matter through which of the many doors we emerged. How he knew which door, and how he achieved such a parking feat in that busy airport, was astonishing.

And nearly always on the ride home he regaled us with

his latest energy-reviving Newfie joke. Probably his best concerned the carpenter working in a busy workshop who suddenly exclaimed, "I've cut off my ear!" Immediately, he and his mate dropped to their knees and began searching in the sawdust and shavings for the dismembered ear. Within seconds his pal stopped searching and asked, "Is this it?"

"No," answered the carpenter. "Mine's got a pencil stuck behind it."

NEWFOUNDLAND SALVATIONISTS are a special breed, possessing the kind of zeal and fervor one associates with the earliest days of the Army. A rousing chorus will not be sung just once or twice in meetings, but repeated six or seven times, the pace increasing each time. Testimony time, when members of the congregation tell how they are faring in the good fight of faith, usually lasts for at least half an hour. Indeed, the attenders will feel cheated if the evening meeting closes before 9 p.m.—especially if they are out before the Pentecostals!

Fine Army bands and songster brigades give great service in the major towns, but in the outport corps the singing pulses along to the rhythmic beat of accordions, guitars and drums. Men's fellowships are especially strong, comprising members whose physique advertises their occupation as fishermen, or in the lumber, hydro-electric or mineral mining trades. Their faith and their practical service are as strong as their physique. They love to recount stories both ancient and modern concerning Army life. Remembering my own advice, I'll not try to retell any, but let Major Cecil Cooper, a fine Newfoundlander himself, recall some from his own experience:

Late one night I was called to the hospital at Corner Brook. There was a lady who had come to the city from one of the outports. I found that she was really quite depressed and nervous and obviously somewhat shy. As I was trying to counsel her, a nurse came in and seeing me there said to the lady, "Is this your husband?" The patient's bashfulness seemed to vanish and she answered the nurse quickly and quite seriously, "My goodness, no. Things are bad enough as they are."

Brigadier Charlie Hickman was in Green Bay conducting a week of nightly meetings in several corps in the area. He and supporting officers traveled from place to place by boat. It was in the fall and though the meetings began in daylight, it was quite dark by the time they ended. However, weather conditions were in their favor, being calm with a nightly full moon.

Before starting the testimony period at one corps, the Brigadier announced that there would be time for a goodly number of folk to speak since they could not start out for home until the moon came up. The meeting went along extremely well with lots of joyful singing and a general sense of rejoicing.

The spirit of elation so affected one old soldier that when he stood to his feet he began his witness by saying, "Brigadier, this meeting is so good I could stay here all night. I hope the moon doesn't come up 'till daylight!"

During testimony time in a small corps meeting, we were singing repeatedly the chorus, "Bright crowns there are, bright crowns laid up on high." With a sense of great elation, one lady stood to her feet and declared, "My comrades, I am not so much caring about the bright crowns. If I make it, they can put an old enamel pan on my head!"

Six months after a new Commanding Officer had been appointed to one of the large outport corps, an old soldier who was not blessed with all his faculties was heard to declare, "Boy, we got some officer here this time. I've been saved thirteen times already!"

A lady who had not previously attended an Army meeting wandered into an outport corps. Some of the songs they were singing had rather a fast beat and she could not quite catch all the words. But she was sure she had got at least one song right. During the following week on one hot day she went through the house opening the windows and astonished her husband by singing constantly, "Hoist the winders, hoist the winders all." On inquiry of a Salvationist, the husband later learned the correct words: "I surrender, I surrender all."

An officer, visiting an elderly couple who had never been believing Christians, began tactfully to suggest to them that the light of the gospel would transform their lives and understanding. He began: "You know, you dear folk are in a sense living in darkness." The old lady nodded her head in agreement and replied: "I told John we should put another window in the kitchen."

It was during the days when many people in Newfoundland were getting rid of wood and coal stoves, and buying oil ranges. The young corps officer was trying to convince his corps local officers that they ought to purchase an oil range for the quarters. The frugal corps treasurer was adamant. "No, Lieutenant, the corps cannot afford to buy a stove at the present time." "But treasurer," protested the officer, "if we buy one of these ranges, we'll save half the fuel bill."

To which the treasurer replied, "In that case, let's buy two and save all the fuel bill."

I was to conduct a wedding during my early days as an officer. The couple did not think it necessary to have a rehearsal a day or two before the ceremony. Reluctantly, I gave way on condition that they arrived early for the service so I could give them instructions about the processional. They arrived in good time. Concerning the ceremony, I indicated it was only a matter of them repeating exactly the wording I spoke.

I began with the nervous groom and said to him in a whisper, "Repeat after me." He replied in a whisper, "Repeat after me." Attempting to put him straight, I said, "Not quite yet." He repeated, "Not quite yet."

Needless to say, we had to have a consultation.

An officer was summoned to the hospital late at night to console a man who was to have major stomach surgery the next morning. On arrival, the officer realized the man was nervous, tense and afraid. "What really is the cause of your anxiety?" he asked him. The gentleman replied, "I've got to have this stomach operation tomorrow, and truth to tell I haven't got the guts."

Called on to outline Charles Wesley's great atonement hymn, "Would Jesus have the sinner die?" a young officer obviously felt nervous facing a crowd of 4,000 people attending the Congress gathering in St. John's. But he read well and effectively until in the fourth verse he intoned, "The story of Thy love repeat in every sinner's drooping ears."

The Corps Sergeant Major in one of our large corps was a keen grocery merchant. One Sunday evening before we set out for the Sunday evening open-air service, he offered prayer as he usually did. We were to visit the home of an elderly soldier who had been confined to his home for quite a long time. The Sergeant Major began with typical enthusiasm, "O Lord, bless this customer to whom we will minister."

NEWFOUNDLAND HAS MANY HAPPY MEMORIES for Commissioner Edward Read, who served as Provincial Commander there in days when the Army's work on the island came under one top leader. He recalls:

When I arrived in Little Bay Islands one Saturday afternoon, the corps officer asked if I would visit "Uncle Eddie." The Lieutenant explained: "He's a great Salvationist but has been shut in for years. He always appreciates it if a visiting 'special' comes round to see him."

So we made our way down the path to Eddie's little house and found him in bed, as always he had to be, but as cheerful as the C.O. assured me he always was. "So you're the P.C.," he cried, "from England, no doubt?"

"No," I replied, "I'm a Canadian, from Upalong." "Ah, well," said Eddie, "have you heard about the Englishman who came to Newfoundland?" I urged him to go on with a story he obviously relished.

"Well, this Englishman said to the Newfie he met, 'You've got a lot of lakes here in the island.' The Newfie replied, 'No, none. Not a lake at all.' 'But,' countered the visitor, 'I saw several large bodies of water. What are those if they are not lakes?' 'Oh, them,' said the bayman, 'them's ponds. Just ponds.' 'I see,' commented the Englishman. 'So what is a lake in Newfoundland?' 'Lakes? Lakes? Over here them's when you get a hole in your rubber boot!'"

And Eddie roared joyfully over his story, savoring the discomfiture of the mythical Englishman (and of the present Upalonger) and their inability to cope with the niceties of a Newfie's tongue.

I came away wondering if, had I been bedridden for fourteen years, I could have regaled a visitor as amusingly on a Saturday afternoon.

CHAPTER 8

THE SONGS
OF SALVATION

THE POETIC LANGUAGE OF THE CHURCH'S hymnology can fall strangely on the ears of some with limited reading skills or small regard for poetry. They struggle awkwardly to scan the lines and hesitantly stumble over unfamiliar words. But the invitation often given in Salvation Army meetings for any in the congregation to stand and read aloud the verse of a hymn between the congregation's singing of the verses is open to all, the not-so-well-read equally with the well-read. It's a traditional privilege within the "unstructured structure" of their non-liturgical worship that Salvationists treasure.

For, as a line in an Army song says, "Not the rich or learned or clever only shall by Him be rescued," and sometimes those least able to respond are the keenest to seize the opportunity when the invitation, "Who'd like to read a verse?" is given.

Not surprisingly, some hilarious howlers are heard and the proper attempts by listeners to stifle their inward giggles make the faux pas all the funnier. Regular attendees at a corps in Toronto, Canada, have not forgotten the time when a good brother, not familiar with the word "diadem," read "Bring forth the royal didlidum, And crown Him Lord of all."

Brigadier Ivy Waterworth recalls the live-wire bunch—all eight of them—that kept the USA Atlanta Number One Corps on its toes, and each other in what she describes as a state of consecrated chaos. With such a cloud of sibling witnesses, she says one can empathize with young Willy as he stood to line out a song in a young people's legion meeting: "My God, I am thin," he began. (Had anyone actually torn off the "e" from the page?)

Even the two brothers who later became dignified commissioners joined in the uproar that broke up the meeting. They never forgot that night when Richard, Ernest, Edith, Wilson, Nancy, Keitha, David and Edwy Holz, along with the Baldwins, Coxes, Cunninghams and others, convulsed in laughter on the youth hall floor.

Bakersfield, California, is properly named, declares Mrs. Lt.-Colonel Hazel Rice. During summer, the temperature lingers at 100F degrees. She and Gene were appointed corps officers there in mid June. The building had been sold. They were to finance and build a new one. Meanwhile, they worshipped in a store front, 18 x 60 ft. A platform had been erected at one end of the room. The wall behind concealed a kitchen sink, counter and enclosed toilet. ("During the meetings, when someone started forward, we didn't know if they were coming to kneel at the Penitent-form or going to the bathroom!" recalls Hazel.) And there was no air conditioning.

One hot Sunday evening, one of the soldiers was leading a song, reading the verse that ends, "Till each sin-burdened soul finds its rest." Most appropriately and quite innocently, he read, *"Till each sunburned soul finds its rest."*

During the Army's centennial celebrations in London, England, Salvationists from many countries took part in meetings. Doris Martin remembers a young Swedish couple visiting her corps. The husband was astonishingly fluent in English; his wife not so. She gallantly outlined the verse, "I once was an outcast, a stranger on earth," and continued, "A sinner by choice and *a lion by birth.*" It's understandable that she didn't want to call herself an "alien" and no one in the understanding congregation laughed, says Doris.

~~

IT'S AS WELL TO LISTEN INTENTLY to what words tiny tots in Sunday school are actually singing. This compiler has to acknowledge that he was probably at least five before he understood the line from the childhood hymn, "Pity my simplicity." Previously I had sung, "Pity mice in Plicity." After all, it sounds exactly the same. I imagined that Plicity was some sort of nasty cage. Since it was a verse we sang at prayer time, I naturally assumed we were praying for those unfortunate locked-up creatures.

Ray Wiggins asserts that songwriter Gladys Taylor told him she believingly sang, "I am Gladys when I'm loving Thee the best."

Major Clifford Kent was caroling with the band at Sunderland Monkwearmouth in the U.K. when his wife was called in to a home where the lady told how her tiny granddaughter returned from her first carol service singing, "Away in a manger, No crab for his bread."

Yet another childish misinterpretation concerns the chorus, "I will make you fishers of men." It came out, "I will make you vicious old men," which is certainly different.

~~

BUT EVEN WHEN A SONG'S WORDS are correctly read or sung, they can still be totally inappropriate for the occasion. General Albert Orsborn gleefully told of the time he was leaving an Indian territory after several hectic days of speaking in crowded meetings and a succession of private engagements. The campaign had meant a great deal of anxiety both before and during the visit for the local Territorial

Commander, as well as much hard work for his distinguished visitor.

The General was leaving by train for a further campaign in another part of India. The platform was crowded with loyal Indian Salvationists eager to catch a last glimpse of this charismatic leader. He stood at the open window of the compartment and waved to the cheering people, stirred in his heart by such a demonstration of affection. Then laughter engulfed him as the train began to pull out of the station. With a Freudian slip that revealed his inner feelings, the Territorial Commander had struck up the chorus, "Gone is my burden, He's rolled it away." Innocently, all his comrades joined in heartily.

Air travel has done away with most of the histrionic farewells that departing missionary officers used to undergo with as much grace as possible at the London, England, railway stations. Necessary airport security has ruled out those emotional public scenes when not only family and friends, but colleague officers and even congregations, complete with "Blood and Fire" flag, would gather to give those called to "Greenland's icy mountains and India's coral strand" what was called "a good send-off." A white-haired retired Colonel, affectionately known as Daddy Bedford, clad in the red tunic he wore during his own days in India, would supervise the arrangements, being well- known and highly respected by the railway station authorities. At least the well-intentioned "good send-offs" had the effect of making the farewelling officers glad to be on their way!

On the occasion when Commissioner and Mrs. Reginald Woods boarded a train at Liverpool Street Station, en route for Germany, where the Commissioner had been appointed Territorial Commander, most of the staff of the Editorial Department he was leaving stood alongside the train, gazing at their departing boss and his wife. As many as could get near had already clustered around them aboard the train for a last word and a final prayer, watched with interest by other passengers. Now they could just look, gesticulate, try to lip-send a message through the glass of the window, all the time wondering why on earth it was taking so long for the train to go. Finally, the guard blew his whistle. It was a signal for someone immediately to strike up the rousing Army chorus, "We'll never let the old flag fall," though unfortunately pitching it in too high a key. But with a sense of relief that the waiting was at last over, the editorials joined in with fervor.

Slowly the train moved out, only to reveal a jammed-packed platform-full of home-going commuters staring almost face-to-face at the uniformed singing Salvationists. They were waiting for their local train to arrive on the track immediately parallel to that on which the Woods' train had departed. Somewhat self-consciously and still struggling to reach the high notes of the badly pitched chorus, the editorials achieved a sudden diminuendo from fortissimo to pianissimo and slipped away to write more challenging articles on the need for all Salvationists to stand like the brave and give forthright Christian witness to the public.

～

IT WAS TYPICALLY THOUGHTFUL of Mrs. General Wilfred Kitching to realize some days before Christmas that the season of merrymaking might find no echo of joy in the hearts of several women officers serving on the International and Associated Headquarters. They were widows whose husbands had been "promoted to Glory" while on active service and who then had been able to find a fulfilling role themselves in a headquarters appointment. The kind Mrs. Kitching foresaw the possibility that their sense of loss and feelings of loneliness might well be all the keener as they watched other couples enjoying the blessings of the season together.

She sent a personal note to each one, inviting them to join her in a time of friendship and understanding over a cup of tea. Naturally, they sang a carol together. The choice: "As with gladness men of old."

PIANISTS, ORGANISTS AND BANDMASTERS can sometimes be so wrapped up with the beauty of their music that they forget to check whether the words associated with the melody they are playing may possibly be inappropriate for the occasion. I recall attending the service at North Toronto Citadel on a bitterly cold Sunday morning when the organist chose to play for the offertory what was for him just a nice little classical tune, "Where'er you walk, cool gales shall fan the glade." ("You're not kidding, brother," was my unexpressed irreverent thought.)

In that same Canadian city, Mrs. Lt.-Colonel Pearl Putt recalls the day when a newly built residence for retired officers was opened. Once the dedication service was concluded, visitors were invited to tour the premises. The band, recruited for this very special occasion, was there to provide some cheery music. Pearl poked her friend in the ribs. "Do you know what they are playing?" she whispered. The tune was, "You are drifting, drifting to your doom." Needless to say, says Pearl, neither of us was in a hurry to put in our application for residence after that!

It seemed to the late Colonel Wm. G. Harris that a congregation's choice of chorus was adding insult to an injury he had sustained. While en route to conduct a Sunday morning meeting, he was involved in a minor accident. He gallantly determined to fulfill the engagement. Inevitably, he was seriously delayed and the service commenced without him. As he entered, everyone was singing with gusto, "Lord, do it again."

Sometimes a totally unexpected happening, even a moment of high drama, can panic a meeting leader and make him or her alight on a totally inappropriate song or chorus to smooth over the happening. Such was the case at Shepherds Bush Corps, in West London, where officer cadets from the International Training College were presenting one in their weekly series of drama items based on Bunyan's *Pilgrim's*

Progress. A matinee "Joy Hour" for children was followed by an evening showing for adults.

The cadets wanted to add as much realism as possible to the scene where Pilgrim confronts the fearful Apollyon, that "foul fiend coming over the field to meet him." A row of lit candles on the rather barren stage offered the opportunity for Apollyon to spit fire from his mouth with spirit. But the "foul fiend" himself caught fire. Fellow cadets swiftly wrapped his cloak around him to extinguish the flames. The stage curtains were immediately closed. The watching London children—never the easiest to control—were agog with excitement.

Cadet Eric Munford, the "Joy Hour" leader, leapt into action. "Let's sing a chorus, children," he announced: "See this little light of mine."

Sometimes there are overtones to a song title that become significant only when announced in a public assembly. Commissioner Ed. Carey tells me that a fellow salvation soldier of his at Asbury Park, New Jersey, still vividly remembers a songster brigade rehearsal when she lived in Liverpool, England. The songster leader had been a widower for a considerable time but eventually the glad day came when he found a new love. At the first songster practice on his return from honeymoon, he announced the selection to be rehearsed: "Gone are the nights of loneliness." He seemed astonished at the gales of laughter which greeted his announcement.

A house of ill repute in Camberwell, England, certainly needed the witness of devout cadets from the International Training College outside its doors. But such an establishment also needed very careful choice of street meeting content. Major Arthur J. Brown recalls that such sensitivity was obviously lacking when a young man cadet strode forward into the ring of cadets and vociferously read out the Charles Wesley hymn lines: *Come, O thou traveler unknown, Whom still I hold but cannot see…with Thee all night I mean to stay And wrestle till the break of day."* Perhaps it is not surprising that this great hymn of the church was omitted from the 1986 revision of "The Song Book of The Salvation Army."

IT WAS NO FAULT OF JIMMY, our color sergeant, that he was unable to read or write, relates Major Arthur J. Brown. His education had been completely neglected in the more remote reaches of County Antrim, Northern Ireland. It was all the more credit to him that after his Christian conversion he not only attended the open-air meetings but was on the list of leaders.

True, he had only two outlines or programs, but these were learned by heart. He also subscribed to the idea that since, as the Army's doctrines declare, ALL Scripture is given by inspiration of God, then ANY Scripture is suitable for reading in a street meeting.

So it was that on one occasion he turned to Mrs. Brown, presented her with a Bible opened at a long list of "begats," and asked her to read the selected passage. Audrey rose to the occasion. "There's a lot of hard words here, Jimmy," she said. "Can I choose an easier passage?" Jimmy indicated that this was quite acceptable.

But it could only have been Jimmy who stood in the street one Sunday morning holding forth determinedly despite the sudden deluge that fell from what had been an azure-blue Irish sky. As the first big drops bounced off the roadway, so every bandsman and soldier scattered to the comparative shelter of the doorways, leaving Jimmy oblivious to their deserting him.

With the rain dripping from him, he sang at the top of his voice: "Mercy drops round us are falling, but for the showers we plead."

What a loyal soldier of Christ!

MISCHIEVOUS, CREATIVE MINDS find wonderful material for parody in all hymns, as the greatly loved missionary officer, Canadian Colonel Burton Pedlar, early found in his career. As a young Captain he was enjoying serving in

Sault Ste. Marie, Ontario, and really felt he had great rapport with the youth of the area. One night, as he made his way to his Army hall, he was delighted to hear the young folk singing enthusiastically to the beat of a guitar. He thought they were being especially inspired as he heard them singing, "Take your burden to the Lord and leave it there." On getting nearer he heard more clearly the words: *"Take your Burton to the Lord and leave him there."*

For almost one hundred years The Salvation Army's own printing house, The Campfield Press, enjoyed a deserved reputation for high quality and efficiency in Britain. Locally, in the old Roman city of St. Albans, it also had a deserved reputation for upholding Christian ideals, including that of holding a weekly, short, mid-day devotional service, addressed by local ministers and visiting Army officers. Major Frederick Coutts, one day to become General, established a reputation for himself by the excellence of his down-to-earth, free-from-jargon, topical speaking at these gatherings. (A collection of his talks was published under the title, *In the Dinner Hour.*)

Each Wednesday afternoon, when employees returned from their lunch break, the first fifteen minutes were spent attending the service—a quarter of an hour for which, of course, they were paid. No complaints about that. Less popular was the practice of closing the entrance door where workers clocked in at a given hour shortly before the service commenced, this to avoid disturbing the devotions. Thus latecomers would find themselves "just outside the land of promise" and losing a few shillings in their pay-packet at the end of the week. That was not quite so popular, as they made plain in protests to the then Assistant Managing Director, Colonel Wm. Pritchard.

What was popular on juke boxes and radio stations at that time was a song, "Open the door, Richard, and let me in." It had to happen, of course. The Wednesday following their protest, a small group of late arrivers serenaded the devotional congregation through the letter-box: "Open the door, Pritchard, and let us in."

As former Composing Room Overseer, Fred Norton reminds me, not far from The Campfield Press was the Crown Hotel, a place for liquid refreshment for those of such inclination as well as accommodation. Occasionally, a visiting meeting leader would choose the song, "O happy, happy day, when old things passed away!" It was a popular choice with many of the employees, as one could see when an impish grin spread over their faces. For verse 2 begins, "I laid my burden down, And started for the Crown."

The same Fred Norton likes to remember Sundays at St. Albans Corps when he and his fellow young people's band members felt rather cheated if there was not a rousing "wind-up" to the day—a kind of salvation jollification and praise. But for some living a distance from the hall in days of no country bus service and owning no cars, the extra long meeting was not for them. On one occasion when the Commanding Officer noticed the Corps Secretary buttoning up his coat and about to set out on the long journey home, he called out, "Just before you go, Secretary, give us your testimony, please."

Still struggling with his coat, the Secretary burst into song: "I'm a soldier, bound for Glory, I'm a soldier going home." Amidst much laughter he called out, "Good-night everybody!" The Captain took the cue. "It's time to follow the Secretary's example." He pronounced the benediction.

CHAPTER 9

THESE ARE OUR PEOPLE

EVEN SUCH A HIGHLY REGIMENTED organization as
The Salvation Army occasionally produces officers who,
with wide-eyed innocent naiveté, do the totally unexpected
thing. They live in a dream world of high idealism and total
impracticality. As with absent-minded professors, the stories
about them are legion.

Just to mention the name of Major Courtland Moore in
the USA Southern Territory is to evoke a string of stories
beginning, "Remember when old Courtland…"

Courtland began his officership as he was to continue over
the many years. He arrived at the School for Officer Training
in Atlanta, Ga., wearing a brown suit, to the amazement of his
colleague cadets, all stiffly clad in their smart new navy blue.
"Why aren't you wearing uniform?" they demanded to know.

Courtland's innocent blue eyes opened wide. "I-I didn't
know," he explained with the injured look of a lad who would
be the last to cause offense. "I thought officer-training would
be like attending a Bible conference."

Courtland seemed to be strongly attached to his old brown suit. He appeared in it again quite soon after the training session commenced. His cadet brigade had been told it would be going that evening to the men's social. Once again his cadet colleagues asked why he wasn't in uniform.

And once again the blue eyes opened wide. "Do you mean we have to wear uniform to go to a party?" he asked with amazement. "I thought a men's social would be a party."

No party indeed, they told him. He was to give a hand with some very down-to-earth jobs at the men's social work hostel.

The cadet who thought officer training would be like attending a Bible conference admits to having quite a passion for Bible conferences. In his imaginative way he decided one year that he, his wife and family could combine attendance at a Florida Bible conference with a holiday. They set off for this dual vacation in their transit van.

Courtland's plan was that his children should enjoy the glories of the Sunshine State's parks while he and Mrs. Moore attended the conference. Then at night they would all sleep in the van on Daytona Beach. The first night, the children settled comfortably inside the van. Courtland and his wife climbed up on to a mattress on the top of the van beneath a mosquito net, held at each corner by a dowel fixed to the van.

With the ocean's lullaby and the warm gentle breezes to lull them, sleep came quickly to the tired family. So did the police. Courtland awakened to the flashing of the police car beams and the arm of the law shaking his. "You can't stay here, you know, sir," said the officer kindly.

Always eager not to offend authority, Courtland—in his pajamas —slid quickly off the van roof *without waking his wife* and into the driving seat. She woke up, dear girl, to discover the world and the mosquito net flying past her as Courtland revved up the engine to 50 mph to get off the 45-degree-angle sand dune behind which they had parked.

Later that day she was heard murmuring repeatedly, "O Courtland, dear Courtland."

A man with such a heart of gold and a total absence of worldly wisdom has always been a soft touch for the unscrupulous. At the Dallas Social Centre, they all knew that kind Major Courtland would respond to a sob story, no matter how preposterous. For instance, ne'er-do-wells would plead to borrow his truck for some concocted emergency. Courtland rarely refused, as the steadily worsening state of his vehicle testified. The vehicle became such a wreck that Divisional Commander Major John Mikles told him to get rid of it. It was a menace on the roads and a threat to the Army's insurance coverage.

The ever respectful Courtland did not argue. "I'll put it up for sale right away," he promised.

Less than a week later, Courtland reported that he had found a buyer. Could he have just a few minutes off to deliver it to the nearby purchaser? "Certainly," replied the relieved D.C.

Three hours later the visibly annoyed Colonel was wanting to know where on earth Courtland had got to. Finally he returned.

"It was only a couple of blocks away," declared Courtland, "but you see, sir, the wheels would only turn right, and right, and right."

It almost goes without saying that Courtland Moore's reputation in the USA Southern Territory as one who loves his Lord and his fellow-men is unsurpassed.

<hr />

Salvation Army officers do not usually address larger audiences in their retirement years and achieve more publicity than in their active service. But Commissioner Catherine Bramwell Booth, granddaughter of William and Catherine Booth, surely did. At the age of 94 she was voted (to her great amusement) "Speaker of the Year" by the Guild of Professional Toastmasters in Britain; appeared three times on television (reprimanding one interviewer for his lack of general knowledge); broadcast twice on radio; started writing her fifth book; wrote a strong letter to the London *Times* on the subject of children and sex; and addressed a public

Salvation Army meeting for two hours without sitting and without notes.

Interlacing all her speaking was an impish humor, as many a media interviewer learned to their chagrin. What sometimes seemed to be the innocent question of a little old lady usually proved to be a witty barb that rocked an audience to laughter and applause. No one knew better than Commissioner Catherine the power of humor.

In December 1982, she and her two sisters—Major Dora, then aged 89, Colonel Olive, aged 91, and Commissioner Catherine anticipating her 100th birthday in July, 1983—appeared on Russell Harty's highly popular weekly TV chat show. As the live audience gave excited applause to three sisters of such vintage, Russell Harty wanted to be sure each was sitting in the assigned chair so he knew the identity of each. "Now, let me be sure," he said. "You are Major Dora and you are Colonel Olive and you are Commissioner Catherine…"

Commissioner Catherine cut in on him. "Yes we are. And who are you?" she asked, with seeming sweet innocence. The audience went wild at this debunking of the great man.

More was to follow. "Tell me," asked Harty, "if your famous grandfather, the Army's Founder, were alive today, would he have come with you tonight on television?" Catherine's reply was startlingly swift. "No," she answered at once.

"Why not?" said the astonished Harty.

"Because he would have been busy doing something more important," shot back Catherine. Again the audience was convulsed with laughter.

But, yes, he would have used television, went on the Commissioner, for he was a bit of a showman. "You know what that means?" she added, with another innocent sly dig.

"Er, yes, I do," laughed Harty, realizing he was having his leg pulled and was no match for the lady in the poke bonnet.

~~~

COLONEL BERNARD ADAMS, BANDMASTER of the international staff band for twenty-eight years and its cornet soloist for twelve years before that, was notorious for his dry, poker-faced wit. He was a natural musician, incisive with the baton and with the kind of flexible embouchure which made him immediately proficient on any brass instrument. A bass player who complained in rehearsal that the manuscript in front of him was unplayable received a salutary object lesson when the Bandmaster asked him for his instrument and immediately deftly performed the "unplayable."

However, successive editors of *The Musician* tried in vain to persuade this gifted man to put pen to paper and share his wide knowledge. One editor, Lt.-Colonel Sidney Williams, felt he had finally broken through this wall of literary silence when Bernard agree to answer readers' questions on cornet playing.

The Musician proudly announced: "Army's most noted cornet player will answer your questions."

A deluge of inquiries was expected. Surprisingly, at first none came. Then the first request arrived: "How can I develop a tone like Willie Lang's?"—a well-known cornetist in a non-Army contest band. Sid Williams directed it to Bernard without delay.

His reply came quickly: *"Tell him to write and ask him!"*

A later editor, Colonel Brindley J. Boon, felt he might be more successful if he used the telephone to ply the great man with a question from a bandsman in the north of England. It appeared the inquirer lived in a heavily industrialized area and his precious brass instrument was constantly being tarnished by the noxious atmosphere. Was there any cure for his problem?

By this time, Colonel Adams was manager of the Musical Instrument Department at the Army's Trade Headquarters and head of the factory where Army band instruments were crafted by hand. Explaining the dilemma, Brindley 'phoned the Colonel to ask if there was anything the bandsman could do.

"Oh yes," he answered immediately. "Great," responded Brindley, "hang on while I get a pen...Now, what can he do?"

"Move," said Bernard, replacing the receiver.

DURING the Staff Band's weekend visit to Cradley Heath, the chairman chosen for the Saturday evening program was the conductor of a local brass band. He was highly complimentary about the Salvationists' playing and said how much he felt his own band had in common with the I.S.B. Indeed, he thought it a great pity that Salvation Army bands and the many other bands in the country did not mix together more and share in concerts.

Bernard Adams picked up his baton to conduct the next piece of music; then, pausing, turned to the congregation and said: "I thank the chairman for his kind words. Concerning his suggestion that we share together more often, there's a fine opportunity tomorrow morning to join us in our open-air meeting at 10 a.m."

THE International Staff Band, despite the players' commitment to the highest concert standards and audiences' critical expectations, never shirks the rigors of open-air meetings in a British climate and lip-fatiguing street marches. Sometimes, staff bandsmen suspect that their hosts like to test "these softies from London" with a punishing route march and heavy outdoor schedule.

During a weekend visit to the Welsh valleys, the Sunday morning street witness took them past fields where the only spectators were the grazing sheep. The absurdity of the program was captured completely in the way Staff Bandmaster Adams called out the next hymn-tune to be played.

Timing each word exactly on the off-beat, so it was heard clearly between the tread of the marching men, he announced in a feigned Welsh accent: "Three-nought-sev'n, 'Bread-of-Heav'n,' two slices." Any feelings of resentment about the futility of the marching exercise evaporated completely in the chorus of laughter.

BERNARD didn't confine his subtle wit only to public occasions. One lunchtime Major Ray Bowes, his deputy bandmaster (and successor in due time), resolved to arrive early for the band's mid-day rehearsal. He was in a contemplative mood and wanted to eat alone before the International Headquarters canteen became crowded. He took his milk, apple, roll and cheese to an empty table.

But to his regret, someone beckoned him over. He politely joined them in conversation, then went to regain his empty table. Further annoyance. Bernard Adams was seated in front of his milk, apple, roll and cheese. Ray greeted the Bandmaster courteously, sat down, then reached over and took the milk, apple, roll and cheese.

Adams watched with impassive face, then dryly asked, "Do you want my overcoat as well?"

"Pardon," said Bowes, with bewilderment. "I-I don't understand..." but his voice faded in *aba aba* sounds.

Then he saw the grinning faces of other staff bandsmen at a nearby table who had realized what had happened. He had gone back to the wrong table. Both bandmaster and deputy had chosen the identical lunch.

MENTION THE NAME OF COMMISSIONER Andrew S. Miller to Salvationists in any part of the USA—or to many church congregations, numerous Rotary clubs, all kinds of conference centers—and the reaction is immediate: "Oh, Andy! What a great guy!"

A committed jogger, he uses his unfailing early morning run to greet every person he meets with a hearty, "Good morning, God bless you!" Like a magnet amidst iron filings, he regularly attracts the oddest happenings. One startled old lady whacked him with her handbag, fearing he was up to no good.

As a member of the Army's 1986 High Council—the exclusive group of Army leaders whose sole duty is to elect the General—Andy still found time to jog along the streets surrounding the Sunbury Court Conference Centre. Outside the Kempton Park Race Course, his "God bless you" earned him an offer of employment.

"Just a minute," said the man. "We've got a caravan show this weekend. I still need a couple of chaps to help in the catering department."

The Commissioner, head of The Salvation Army in the U.S.A. Southern Territory, thanked him warmly for recognizing his likely potential for such basic service. However, he was already gainfully employed.

BUT Andrew is also a jogger of consciences, a highly effective jogger of any audience beginning to slumber before he rises to speak, and a jogger of any rut-routine irrelevance that he believes lessens his own Christian witness and that of his beloved Army. Preaching or describing the Army's compassionate ministry, he will usually speak for thirty minutes, invariably without notes.

Some 900 guests attended a springtime luncheon in the Royal York Hotel, Toronto, Canada, which Commissioner Miller had agreed to address. It was the launching of the annual Red Shield Appeal and Andy was in magnificent form: spellbinding, emotion-stirring. Inevitably, he stressed the duality of the Army's spiritual mission and social service.

Before he could leave the head table, a sophisticated lady hurried to him, gushing her compliments over him. "Oh, Commissioner, you were wonderful. May I beg a favor? Could I have a copy of your notes?"

"Most certainly, ma'am," replied the ever-courteous, smiling Andy. Fiddling inside his fob pocket, he produced a bus ticket on which were written four headings and handed it to her. "There they are," he said apologetically, "but you are most welcome to them." He didn't offer to autograph them. There would have been no room.

SOME of the worldly wisdom that Commissioner Andrew Miller applied to his more than forty years of Salvation Army officership he assuredly owes to his previous years in the U.S. Navy.

As a young Captain, eager to expand the Army's ministry to needy people in Akron, Ohio, he planned a major appeal campaign one Christmas, making full use of the traditional kettles manned by bell-ringers in shopping malls and streets. The shops, stores and large retail outlets mostly welcome the kettles, for they add to the festive atmosphere and increase the shoppers' spirit of generosity.

Manning one of the kettles himself, the young Captain Miller was surprised when a police patrolman bore down on him and directed him to quit, taking his kettle, his bell and himself off the street. There had been a protest about the kettles and the bells. He must go.

Immediately, Captain Miller was full of concern for the patrolman. He understood fully that a patrolman had to do his duty, no matter how unpleasant it was for him. He would try to help him as much as he could. "However," continued Andy, "although I do respect and admire you, I have to let you know that I am not able to move the kettle because I am not the final word on Salvation Army affairs in Akron. You see, I report to a Lt.-Colonel Ted Carey in Cleveland. I shall have to talk to Colonel Carey in Cleveland before I can move my kettle."

"My instructions are to move you right away," began the patrolman again, "and I am asking…"

"I do understand," cut in the Army Captain, "and I do respect and admire you for doing your duty even when you don't personally want to move me on, but you see I have to contact Colonel Carey in Cleveland…"

Wearying of what he could see would be an endless discussion that was getting nowhere, the patrolman moved away. He was followed shortly afterward by a police sergeant. His message was brief and brusque, emphasized by swear-words that were not new to the former navy man. The Captain and his kettle should move fast if he didn't want something to happen to his exterior and posterior. Again Captain Miller was all sweetness and light. He knew that the sergeant really loved the Army and didn't want to spoil Christmas for truly needy people, but he just couldn't move that kettle until he'd spoken with Colonel Carey in Cleveland. Would the sergeant like to man the kettle and ring the bell while he telephoned the Colonel?

As he strode away, the sergeant was still saying in colorful language what he would like to do with the kettle.

When a chauffeur-driven police car containing a lieutenant in charge of the city's traffic department pulled up beside his kettle, Andy knew he had really aroused interest in his Christmas appeal. The white-gloved police lieutenant was smooth, well-educated and charming, the product of a school where they taught law enforcement officers how to handle troublesome people with class and style.

That class and style were fully evident as he spoke with quiet dignity to the Army Captain about the need for him to move on. In a most subservient and apologetic tone, he advised the Army man that unless his kettle was off the street by 3 o'clock the next afternoon, he could look forward to spending the Christmas season in jail.

As soon as Andy could get to the local newspaper, the *Akron Beacon Journal,* he was giving the editor a detailed account of his adventures with the law enforcement officers. Next morning, a headline and report told the story and invited all readers to be present for the arrest of the Salvation Army Captain.

The early-day television crews, with their heavy cameras, radio commentators and newspaper reporters gathered, together with a crowd of several hundred. They were in light-hearted mood and filled Andy's kettles repeatedly. At 3 p.m., everyone looked for the police. At 3:30 p.m. everyone cheered and decided that the police had thought better of their threat.

The Christmas appeal was one of the best ever in Akron, and they expressed their thanks to God and the Chief of Police for their victory in the January annual meeting. The highlight came when Captain Andrew Miller called the police chief to the podium and presented to him the "NO-BELLS PRIZE" for peace on the streets.

LIKE the Lord he loves, Commissioner Andrew Miller has a tender heart for sinners and is much more likely to be understanding of them than condemnatory. When he and his ever-patient wife, Joan, were the officers in charge of Dover, Ohio, they struck up a friendship with a fight promoter named George and his Mennonite wife, Katy. Aside from promoting fights, George and his wife ran an attractive little diner on the corner of 3rd and Tuscarawas Streets.

When George died of a heart attack, Katy asked if Andy would conduct his funeral service. But the Mennonites were not happy about this, for they were critical of George's lifestyle, and decided they would conduct the service. Andy could conduct the cemetery committal service.

Andy recalls: "During the service, I had never before heard such a straight-out recitation of a man's sins at his own funeral. It angered me. I was upset because poor George was not all bad, although the things that were being said about him were basically true. He drank heavily, he smoked, he was unfaithful from time to time, he promoted tough fights. But no mention was made of his many good points. By the time I got to the cemetery, my heart was very much moved and I decided that in my prayer I would offer an eulogy to my pal, George."

It was a rain-soaked day. The casket was held by canvas holders over the open grave. Andy perched with some difficulty on the slippery planks alongside. He gave energetic emphasis to his prayer as he extolled what he felt were George's virtues and commended his pal to God's mercies. With a crack that could have been the answering voice of the Almighty, a plank split and the loving Army man felt himself slithering under the casket. He held his head back as he went on passionately praying for Katy who had lost her partner. Even as he declared his faith in a God who loved and cared for people, who would know that in George there was a tenderness and beauty that belied his actions, so Andrew went further under.

With the "Amen," the funeral director put his head under the covers. In kind but unceremonious language he whispered, "Cap., you're in a hell of a shape." "I understand my shape," answered Andy, "just stop talking and pull me out."

As he emerged, Andy was covered in mud from chest to feet. With all the dignity he could muster, he walked over to Katy, carrying with him the nation's flag, which some members of the armed forces had brought to the burial. They had ceremonially folded it and given it to Andy, for George had been a serviceman.

To quote Andy again: "As I gave the flag to Katy, she said gently to me in the sweetest kind of Mennonite brevity, 'Captain, I love you.' I said, 'I love you too, Katy,' and then I slushed away. Joan had been standing in the back of the crowd while I was doing the committal and she had hurried to the car. We laughed so hard going home, we had a hard time staying on the road."

IF THE HEART of Commissioner Miller is moved by sinners, it is equally stirred by young people. As a Divisional Youth Secretary in Cincinnati, Ohio, assisting Major William Chamberlain, his Divisional Commander, he frequently led meetings for children and always gave opportunity for them to make a personal decision to follow Christ, no matter how young they were.

On one occasion, when he gave the invitation for any child to step forward and kneel at the altar, a large number responded. He had not enough helpers to pray individually with each child, so he invited the youngsters to repeat a prayer, line by line, after him as he prayed.

"Dear Lord Jesus," he began.

"Dear Lord Jesus," repeated the children earnestly.

"Make me a good boy."

"Make me a good boy," echoed the youngsters.

Then, realizing there were girls also among those kneeling, Miller quickly added, "Or a good girl if I happen to be one."

And all at the altar responded, "Or a good girl if I happen to be one."

TEENAGERS RESPOND to the Commissioner's rugged realism and language shorn of religious clichés. One morning, as he led a Bible study with a group of older teenagers in

Salvation Lass: "Are you saved?"
Young man: "No, I am a reporter!"
Salvation Lass: "Oh, I beg your pardon."

"We've all done our bit, the Trotskyists, Marxists, Stalinists, Maoists—now what about some action from The Salvation Army?"

Britain's "winter of discontent" in the late 1960s provided much ammunition for the cartoonists still to see the funny side. Reproduced by courtesy of JAK and the *Lancashire Evening Post.*

"DEAR MR HEALEY
HAS SPARED US"

When Britain's Minister of Defense, Mr. Denis Healey, announced the first of several manpower cuts in the three armed services, the *Daily Mail* printed this "tongue in cheek" cartoon by JON alongside its news report. Courtesy of the *Daily Mail.*

Surely the oldest "joke" to confront Salvationists the world over. Popular among the bawdy postcards usually on sale at seaside resorts for dispatch home by holiday-makers. In the H.B. Series, printed in Holland.

"Deposé"

A send-up of early-day Salvationists in Germany. The French word "deposé" suggests they are being ejected by the police.

Cartoonist Len Norris wonderfully and humorously recognizes the Army's dual ministry of "Heart to God and Hand to Man." Len kindly grants permission to publish his cartoon and sends best wishes. Print by courtesy of *The Vancouver Sun*.

"The brasses tend to dominate and the percussion is over-emphasized in this passage.... but their soup is excellent."

An immediate post-World War II cartoon by Ilingworth. The "Army band" holding an open-air meeting comprises France's President de Gaulle (cornet), USSR Premier Josef Stalin (drum) and Foreign Secretary Molotov (cornet), U.S. President Franklin D. Roosevelt (bass), and Britain's Foreign Secretary Anthony Eden (cymbals). Welcoming neutral countries into the indoor Victory Festival is Britain's Prime Minister, Winston Churchill. One neutral isn't cooperating. Courtesy the *Daily Mail*.

One of a series of impressions drawn by F. Bersch depicting people to be seen on the streets of Berlin. It was published as an ALT-Berlin card by Kunst und Bild, 1 Berlin 61. A USA Western Territory officer used the card in 1993 to send Christmas greetings, over the wording, "Joy to the World!"

Sunday school, the conversation became intimately personal as each of the youngsters acknowledged a deep desire to become a born-again Christian.

"This is a beautiful moment in your lives," said Andy as he prayed with them, "but I believe we should seal these decisions boldly in public. I believe you will want to ratify these decisions by kneeling at the altar in the adult holiness meeting which follows." He suggested that when the invitation was given toward the close of the service, to help them, he himself would move forward and then they would join him at the altar. The young people agreed.

Cadets from the School for Officer Training had been invited to lead the holiness meeting. A young woman cadet had been chosen by the school to preach. She had decided to speak out very boldly about the incursion of the world into the church. As she moved into the field of immorality, Andy's apprehension grew. "I could not believe such a sweet young lady could know about such things," recalls Andy. Step by step, she denounced those who treated the marriage vow lightly and denounced the adultery which she believed was all too common.

As she concluded her address she declared, "Now, let those who need to seek God's forgiveness step forward to the altar."

The moments of total stillness and tension were broken only by the sound of Major Andrew Miller making his way to the altar. Bandmaster Eddie Lowcock let out a groan of "O God, no," as Andy walked by. For at least three minutes, the laughter choked teenagers left Andy to his embarrassing lonely vigil before—with barely suppressed merriment—they clustered around him. There can be little doubt that in heaven the Lord Himself was smiling.

THE COMMISSIONERS and Chief Secretaries of the four USA Salvation Army territories meet in conference with the National Commander and National Chief Secretary at National Headquarters three times a year (*Note: NHQ was located in New York City from 1896-1982. From 1982-1990, it was located in Verona, New Jersey, and it was moved to its present location in Alexandria, Virginia, in 1991.)* To walk down a New York street or worse, to travel on the subway with Colonel Andrew Miller, Chief Secretary of the Central Territory, was always an adventure. Homeward-bound New Yorkers, trying to isolate themselves behind newspapers and magazines in crowd-packed trains, abruptly had their peace shattered as this lover of all humanity stepped aboard. Each would receive a beaming smile and a "God bless you" whether they wanted it or not. Cheerful conversations well above the roar of the subway train would ensue.

I well recall when Colonel John Paton of the Southern Territory, Andrew from the Central, and I representing the West were returning to our hotel after having bought some bagels near Madison Square Garden. As we ascended on an escalator, a man going down the other side, seeing our uniform, called across, "Hi! Do you know Andy Miller?" "Sure," Andy bellowed back. "Wait at the top," yelled the man.

We did. Breathlessly, the man began to eulogize the Brigadier Andy Miller he had known. A wonderful man. A marvelous man. Where was he now? "He lives in Chicago," Andy replied, "and I'll see him tomorrow. Give me your card and I'll let him know we met you. I'm certain he'll drop you a note."

On another occasion, as I strolled along West 14th Street with Andrew, an inebriated man rushed toward us and kicked his leg. "Hey, hey, what's the matter, friend...?" began Andrew, but even as he spoke, two cops leapt from a passing police car and held the drunk. Was there divine protection for this servant of the Lord, I wondered? "Let him be, he meant no harm," pleaded Andy. President George Bush himself could not have more eloquently pleaded for a gentler, kinder America.

~~

THE MEASURE of Commissioner Miller's reputation is shown by the number who have their own stories to tell about him. I choose three from the many:

Commissioner Andrew Miller started for home in his car. From the back seat, where a man had concealed himself,

Andy felt what seemed like a gun in his neck. "Keep driving," said the intruder. Miller began talking. "Do you realize how much trouble you can get into if you steal this car? You're a young man. Why ruin your life? Besides, this isn't much of a car anyway. I was just taking in to a garage because of the problems I'm having with it."

"Shut up," said the would-be thief, "I'm taking this car. Get ready to pull over."

"Well, if you must, but let me pray with you first."

Telling Miller to stop at the next corner, the thief leapt out. As he ran he shouted, "Trust me to pick one of those religious nuts."

—*Ed Carey*

While stationed in New York City, Major Andrew Miller called on a local merchant. When their business was done, Miller said, "Would you like to bow your head in prayer a moment? I want to ask God's blessing on you." The business man would have no part of it, telling Andy in no uncertain terms that he was not in need of prayer. But the Army man was gently insistent, explaining it was important to him that he pray about the project they had discussed. "Just a short prayer," he promised.

After the "Amen" the business man smiled slapped Andy on the back and explained, "I didn't close my eyes."

—*Harry Sparks*

Waiting in a hotel lobby, Commissioner Andrew Miller was mistaken for a bellboy by a well-dressed older woman with a lot of heavy luggage. Without explanation, Andy took hold of her cases and, because he keeps himself so physically fit, he accomplished the task in next to no time.

The lady probably still doesn't understand why her generous tip was graciously but firmly declined or why the bellboy so warmly said to her, "God bless you!"

—*William T. Waste*

WHEN THERE IS MERRIMENT IN ITS RANKS, The Salvation Army is emulating its illustrious Founder, General William Booth. He had a ready wit and, as the records show, he used it effectively in his preaching. Indeed, he is on record as claiming to be a comic—which perhaps is not a very good sample of his wit.

In May, 1873, Booth visited Portsmouth to conduct a service in a music hall which the then Christian Mission had rented prior to leasing a more permanent building in Lake Road. As he approached the door, he stopped to greet a man who was obviously keenly interested in the crowd going into the building.

"Are you a Christian?" Booth asked.

"A Christian?" the man challenged. "Do you know who I am? I am the comic in this music hall."

"Well, I'm a bit of a comic myself," answered Booth.

—*Cyril Barnes in* Words of William Booth.

Early-day Salvationists endured riots and physical injury after the Christian Mission changed its name in 1878 to The Salvation Army and took its militant brand of Christianity to the streets. On January 6, 1882, a mob of ruffians one thousand strong resolved to drive the Army out of the City of Sheffield when it was learned that William and Catherine Booth were to lead a procession through their streets. When the Salvationists finally arrived back at the Albert Hall for the public meeting, many were "black as colliers, their bodies bruised and sore." Uniforms were spoiled with blood and egg-yolk, and instruments battered beyond use.

Their General looked at them with pride. "Now is the time to get your photographs taken," he joked.

—*Cyril Barnes in* Words of William Booth

Theodore H. Kitching, one of Booth's secretaries, made a mistake of some kind on one occasion and reported the matter with some apprehension to the General, who could be quite brusque in manner and even seemingly rough and harsh in his judgments.

"What fool made you a major?" snapped the old man, when he learned of Kitching's error.

THK, as he was known, replied with a smile, "Your son, General" (Bramwell Booth, the Founder's Chief of Staff and successor). Instantly, Booth was laughing with delight at his secretary's quick retort.

—*Theo Kitching*

Booth knew the value of lightening his impassioned preaching with a humorous story. His masterly oratory would hold his audiences spellbound, near to tears one moment, then roaring with laughter the next.

He liked to recount a favorite incident concerning a woman of very doubtful character, well-known in the city for her lack of sobriety. Constantly in the hands of the police for being drunk and disorderly, she once appeared in a befuddled state before a magistrate who told her she could take her choice: either go to prison or be remanded to The Salvation Army. Anything seemed better than prison.

Awakening next morning, she demanded to know where she was. "You're with The Salvation Army," she was told.

"Hey, get me out of here," she yelled, "or I'll lose my reputation."

—*Wm. G. Harris in* Sagas of Salvationism

But Booth was not joking in the guidance he gave to his officers in "a little red book," the Orders and Regulations for Officers he produced in 1881:

1) Keep off all doctors, if possible. If seriously ill, communicate with headquarters.

2) Always wear flannel next to the skin.
3) Keep your feet dry. The female officers should wear galoshes in wet or sloppy weather, especially when snow is on the ground.
4) Have a cold bath, or wash down in cold water, every morning on rising. This will prevent you taking cold.

~~

Some unintentional humor arose when the Founder was outlining a song at the commencement of a crowd-packed meeting. There was scarcely a single seat left available. A man moved slowly down the aisle toward the front of the hall, looking along every row for a place. Booth was reading powerfully the first verse of number seventy-seven in the old song book:

Jesus, the Name high over all
"Lawley, get that man a seat!"
In hell, or earth or sky

—*Lyell Rader, D.D., O.F.*

~~

In his Daily Study Bible Series, Dr. William Barclay relates that while on a world tour, British short-story writer, novelist and poet Rudyard Kipling was watching when General Booth came on board his ship. He came aboard to the beating of tambourines, which Kipling's orthodox soul resented. Kipling got to know the General, and told him how he disliked tambourines and all their kindred. Booth looked at him. "Young man," he said, "if I thought I could win one more soul for Christ by standing on my head and beating a tambourine with my feet, I would learn how to do it."

Years later, on June 26, 1907, Booth and Kipling shared in the same truly splendid degree-presentation ceremony at Oxford University. A profusion of royalty, statesmen and prominent personalities were assembled. Kipling became a Doctor of Literature and Booth was granted the degree of Doctor of Civil Law —a degree which U.S. President Bill

Clinton duly received in 1994. Alas, the history books do not tell us if Booth and Kipling took opportunity to discuss further the merits of tambourine playing, either by hand or with the feet.

CHAPTER 10

THE UNREGIMENTED VIEWS OF CHILDREN

NONE NEED FEEL SORRY for the children of Salvationists. True enough, their parents will haul them off to Sunday school and fervently pray they will grow up to be "little angels," But there is a color, a gaiety, a razzmatazz about a flag-waving, tambourine-banging, trumpet-blowing Salvation Army which thrills most youngsters. By comparison, in a child's eyes many other churches are dead in the water.

No wonder early-day Salvationists immodestly sang:
"I'm going to the Army, I'm going to the Army,
I'm going where the biggest blessings flow.
I hear the big drum beating
That calls me to the meeting;
I've got the Army fever
And I must go."

Some children are born with a silver spoon in their mouth. Army kids prefer a cornet mouthpiece. Toddlers will stand on their parents' laps in the meetings and mimic the Bandmaster conducting the songs. Little girls can't get a small tambourine soon enough. It's wise to keep a distance between yourself and their vigorous skin-banging jingle-rattling.

As children of officers, moving every two or three years to a new town and Army corps, my two older brothers, older sister and I felt a proprietary ownership of each center almost as much as our mum and dad did. We would talk knowledgeably among ourselves as to what should be done to improve the band, which cornet player had the best tone and who could triple-tongue the fastest. Instinctively, we knew which Sunday school teacher we liked and which one we couldn't stand at any price.

We knew the lingo, talked about "open-airs" (street meetings), the "D.C." (Divisional Commander, mum and dad's boss) and "the locals" (local officers - Salvationists holding office as Treasurer, Secretary, Corps Sergeant-Major, etc.). It's likely that the first words I learned to say in priority and sequence were "mummy, daddy and the locals," such was their importance to my parents. Well-trained, experienced, hardworking, cheerful, supportive "locals" were a joy to my mum and dad; any of the other kind were a pain and a problem.

When farewell orders came to us from the Divisional Commander, and the first welcome weekend meetings at the new corps were completed, there would be a general air of cheerfulness in our new abode if across the Sunday night supper table (usually the best meal of the day in the hectic rush on the alleged "day of rest") my Lancashire father could say to my Cornish mother, "'Eh, lass, we've got some great 'locals' here." Even in my infancy, I knew father was not talking about the public houses, which mother visited every Friday and Saturday evening to sell *The War Cry*, returning home with her clothes saturated with the smell of smoke and beer.

The locals would be invited to our quarters (as we called our home) periodically to hold "census meetings." (Senior local officers comprise the census board. Their prime duty—indeed officially their only duty—is to look after "the flock" by reviewing all personnel on the several rolls.) My brother

Bram, freckled and cheekier than I, would call them "sense-less meetings." Father rebuked him, but there was a hint of a grin on his face.

Bram's freckled good looks and air of innocence usually helped him escape retribution. But on one occasion even he felt he'd overstepped the mark. The Divisional Commander, no less, and Mrs. Brigadier Wilfred Kitching (one day to be General and Mrs. Kitching) were at the quarters for meals in between conducting the Sunday services. Both were tall, quite heavily built people, and rather dignified. When they stepped into your house you knew you had quite a lot of divisional commander there.

Mrs. Kitching had a habit of saying, "Well, did you ever!" From earlier occasions, Bram had noted that fact. Father was telling a story over the lunch table. We four were sitting as good as gold, mother's watchful eye scanning us constantly, even while providing a meal for eight. Father came to the climax of his story about a rascal whose life had been transformed after being attracted to the meetings and giving his heart to God. As he paused for breath, Mrs. Kitching interjected: "Well, did you ever!"

Up piped Bram in a loud voice: "NO I NEVER, SAW A DONKEY MADE OF LEATHER."

Seven pairs of eyes immediately focused on him. Father glared. Mother's already warm cheeks went crimson. We other three kids giggled. Mrs Kitching's face wore a look which said, "What a strange little boy!"

But back to the census board meetings. For such occasions, our quarters would gleam brighter than ever, thanks to mum's energetic elbow grease. She firmly believed that cleanliness was next to godliness. Her four offspring regarded it as next to impossible. But for the period of the meeting, we were exhorted to be on our best behavior. It was important for "the locals" to see what little angels their "cartridge" giving (the system of pledged weekly contributions) was supporting—if only just!

Such meetings were not without their advantages. I would listen for father's stentorian voice imploring the Almighty to

bless and further the noble efforts of "the locals" and pro-
nouncing the benediction. I would then station myself strategically near the front door, looking a little forlorn but, as the
youngest child of the regiment, suitably sweet and innocent.
If the meeting had gone well, I found this ploy could supple-
ment my limited pocket money quite considerably.

Bandmasters were good for sixpence; Recruiting Sergeants,
three-pence; Corps Sergeant Majors, two-pence; from
Treasurers came a pat on the head and an admonition to grow
up to be a good boy.

⌒

My mother loved children. She had been the Young
People's Sergeant Major (Sunday school superintendent) at
the corps of Bodmin, Cornwall, to which Father had been
appointed as a single young Lieutenant. Throughout their
married life as officers, father wisely left the supervision of
children's activities to her.

Young people's anniversary programs were her specialty.
An item she enjoyed presenting was called, "Napoleon's
Farewell to his Grandmother." First, the chairman would
announce the title, "Napoleon's Farewell to his Grandmother."

There would be a fanfare of trumpets, and to a continu-
ous roll of drums a lad would march from the back of the hall,
wearing formal livery and shining cockade hat. Arriving in
stately fashion on the platform, the drums still rolling but
now ominously subdued, he would slowly unroll a lengthy
piece of parchment, assisted by several courtiers.

"Hear ye, hear ye," he would bellow. "Napoleon's Farewell
to his Grandmother." Another fanfare, more drums. The congregation's interest would begin to climb to fever pitch. All
heads would turn and eyes focus on the back of the hall as the
spotlighted Napoleon grandly marched in, with general's tunic,
pill box hat, hands behind back. The band played the Marseilles.
At center stage he halted and stared at the congregation.

The rolling drums ceased. In the tense silence that followed Napoleon raised his hand, slowly waved to an imaginary

118

figure at the back of the hall, and in a loving tone called aloud, "Ta, ta, Granny!"

My mum thought that moment was magic! She laughed as much as the children did.

~

With their natural innocence and starry-eyed sense of wonder, children the world over can be relied on to "'tell it as it is." No occasion is so sacred, no visitor to home or church is so important, that small boys or girls will not say, without the slightest inhibition, whatever thought comes into their cherubic heads. Parents who have spent two years teaching them to talk will spend the next fifteen trying to get them to shut up.

Little wonder that Jesus Christ declared, "Except ye... become as little children"—totally without guile or pretense—"ye shall not enter into the kingdom of heaven" (Matt. 18:3). Often enough, Salvationist parents wanting to gently lead their children into the Christian faith are left dewy-eyed and wondering at the naturalness with which their youngsters accept spiritual truth.

In their frankness and their naturalness, the faith they have in a God who is their loving Heavenly Father and their trust in a Christ who with laughing eyes enjoys hearing their simple prayers, is so enviably straight-forward and such a rebuke to struggling, questioning, tradition-encrusted adults.

This compiler has thoroughly enjoyed receiving the following anecdotes:

~

What can you do with Christmas cards when the festive season is past? Many Salvationist families have found the answer: they keep them throughout the year and each day during their family prayer time one member takes a card from the pile, reads the message on it and then remembers the sender(s) in prayer.

It was the turn of 5-year-old Andy, the youngest of three children, to take a Christmas card and say a prayer when the

Divisional Commander and Mrs. Lt.-Colonel Gary Herndon visited Andy's parents, Captain and Mrs. Robert Alridge, of Des Moines, Iowa. Andy drew the card that had been sent to the family by General and Mrs. Arnold Brown, then the Army's international leaders.

Andy launched into his prayer: "Dear God, bless General Brown. Help him to get his soldiers all lined up right, all his ships ready and all his planes working properly..."

His mother gently interrupted. "Andy, darling, General Brown is not a military general. He's our general, the general of The Salvation Army."

Andy began again. " Dear Lord, bless General Brown, whatever he does. Amen."

Bob and Judy Lugiano, members of the corps band at Old Orchard, Maine, were making a serious attempt to help their young son Christopher, age 4, understand that Jesus did not live in a far-away place, up above the bright-blue sky. "He lives in your heart," they explained. "Jesus lives inside of you. Right inside you."

Later that day they were having supper together when Bob noticed that their boy was not eating. "Eat up your supper, Christopher," father directed, "like a good boy."

"No," replied the youngster, "Jesus is full."

—*Rowland Hughes*

The ten-year-old son of our corps officers was assigned to play the part of the Angel Gabriel in the nativity play. He was to announce to the shepherds, "Behold, I bring you good tidings of great joy."

The moment of his declaration came, and with it the panic of stage fright. But he was pushed on to the stage, halo off-center, robe disheveled, wings drooping.

For a moment he stood looking at the audience, then he blurted: "HAVE I GOT NEWS FOR YOU!"

—*Ed Carey*

The 120 beds in the Salvation Army children's home in Mexico City are nearly always filled. Major and Mrs. A. Hurtado served there as administrators for five years. When they were appointed to divisional headquarters, they carefully broke the news to their four children that they would be moving to a new home.

The youngest, seven-year-old José, asked his mother, "How are we ever going to pack up all the beds?"

—*Emily Fritz*

Our family had moved to a new neighborhood which was predominantly Roman Catholic. One day, my junior high school daughter and I were at the sink washing up the dishes. She told me that her new friends at school knew hardly anything about The Salvation Army that William Booth had founded in England in 1865. They knew only about the social service trucks and the big thrift stores.

After discussing this for a while, I turned and asked our six- year-old first grader what she said if questioned about her church. She had just started junior soldier preparation classes and was our "shy one," not given to much conversation.

Calmly she replied, "I just tell them I go to Saint William!"

—*Arlee Lansing*

The sweet innocence of childhood was gloriously shown during a singing company rehearsal at Winton, Bournemouth. Asst. Young People's Singing Company Leader Lyndon Bexon was teaching the young folk a new song. Line by line, part by part, sentence by sentence he helped them become familiar with the words and music. Satisfied at last that they had a fair grasp of the composition, Lyndon commanded: "Now, everyone stand up, put it all together and make it sound like a song."

Six-year-old Rhys Bennett, not yet old enough to be commissioned a singing company member and standing just about knee-high to the 6 ft. 4 in. assistant leader towering above him, craned his little neck to gaze up into Mr. Bexon's face and said with all seriousness, "But Lyndon, it *is* a song."

A new baby was expected soon by the Commanding Officer's wife. The visiting Divisional Commander asked the officers' six-year-old son if he was going to have a brother or a sister.

The lad replied: "I don't know. I thought we had to have whatever divisional headquarters sends us!"

—*Ed. Carey*

A Lt.-Colonel Raymond Wood, the Greater New York Divisional Commander, together with his wife, was visiting the quarters of an officer couple. The Woods had just been appointed to leadership of the division and wanted to become quickly acquainted with all their officers .

Shortly after the corps officers had welcomed their new leaders to their quarters, the four-year-old son entered the room. He sidled up to his six-year-old sister and in a stage whisper asked, "Who are they?"

"They're our new disease," he whispered back.

—*Robert E. Thomson*

Our son, Daniel, aged 5, was in kindergarten. When his school announced open house, we, as good parents, decided to attend. We went to our son's classroom and there met his teacher.

As we studied the wall charts telling of the children's progress, we were surprised to notice that, unlike the others, Danny did not have a big star next to his name for knowing the address of where he lived. "There must be some mistake," we said to his teacher. "He surely does know."

The teacher confirmed that Danny had not been able to tell her where he lived. She had done what she could to help him, asking him was it a house, an apartment, a house trailer. But to all her questions, Danny could only keep repeating "No, no, no." All he would say was that it was like a half dollar.

Suddenly light dawned. Between my gurgles of laughter I gave the solution. "I know what he's referring to," I said, "HE LIVES IN THE QUARTERS."

We all had a big laugh about Danny and his complete immersion in Salvation Army phraseology. The teacher immediately put a big star beside his name.

—*Elizabeth Miles*

The Sunday school teacher held the close attention of the young children as she taught them about the wonders of heaven. "Now," she said, "hands up all those children who would like to go to heaven."

Every hand shot up, except for that of one little boy in the front row.

"Don't you want to go to heaven, Billy?" asked the teacher.

"I can't," said the little lad tearfully. "My mom told me I had to go straight home."

A Lieut.-Colonel was to conduct the Sunday night meeting at the corps where we were stationed. He and his wife joined us for supper. At the end of the meal, it was our son's turn to return thanks. He prayed most sincerely, "O Lord, bless the Colonel and tonight help him to preach as good as my dad."

Then there was the officers' child who joined his parents for dinner during the visit of the Field Secretary. Obviously he had heard his mother and father expressing their feelings at having been stationed in small corps long enough. Suddenly, the lad blurted out: "Colonel, when are you going to give my mom and dad a decent corps?"

—*Bob Chapman*

≈

Six-year-old Alistair Boyd, son of Lieut.-Colonel and Mrs. Hugh Boyd, admitted to trombonist Sid Greetham after a Sunday morning meeting at Sheffield Citadel, Yorkshire, that he had intended to "get saved" that morning, but had somehow lacked the courage to go forward and kneel at the Penitent form. Sid suggested to the little boy that he could do so in the afternoon praise meeting. No, responded the lad, it would be too noisy then. Sid tried again. "Well, why don't you get saved at home with just your mummy there?"

"Oh, no," replied Alistair, immediately indignant. "Gregor (his brother) did that and he didn't get saved properly."

—*Ray Wiggins*

≈

Major Annie Carby was on registration duty at a divisional young people's Adventure Day being staged by the Army in Leeds, Yorkshire. Her duty was to note the arrival of each of the young delegates and direct them to the house to which they had been appointed. The name of one of the Army's great Generals had been given to each of the houses: BOOTH, CARPENTER, KITCHING, COUTTS, etc.

A worried ten-year-old lad approached Annie. "Please Miss, I've been put in Carpenter House, but I'm no good at carpentry. PLEASE COULD I GO INTO THE KITCHEN?"

—*Cliff Kent*

≈

Major Hilda Harvey, who gave distinguished service in the United Kingdom's Goodwill Department, had a very soft spot in her heart for the Cockney children who would revel in a week of holiday away from London's slums at the Army's

Sunbury Court Youth Centre. Though, she acknowledged, they could be "little devils," she loved each one and laughed at their typical Cockney wit.

Wanting to teach them in a meeting about the difference between right and wrong, she began with the question: "What sort of children come to Sunbury Court?"

"Good 'uns!" they chorused back at her.

"And what sort of children go to heaven?" she asked.

"Dead 'uns," they yelled back at her delightedly.

—*John Mowat*

En route to the dining hall in the College for Officer Training, a young officer cadet was doing her utmost to reason with her four-year-old daughter about the necessity of washing one's hands before entering and eating. "Why must I wash?" demanded the child. Patiently but firmly the young mother replied, "Because you might have germs on your hands. And, besides, Jesus wants little girls to be clean."

The little tot stamped her foot. "Derms and Desus, derms and Desus. That's all I hear about 'round here and I'm getting tired of boaf of dem."

—*Ben Meyer*

I well remember conducting the meetings at a UK Goodwill Centre some years ago on a Whit Sunday—so called because of the tradition that candidates for baptism on this Pentecost Sunday should wear white garments. Towns and cities in the north of England also had a tradition that on this Sunday the churches—in particular the Sunday-school children—would parade through the streets on a march of witness. The churches would vie with each other as to which looked the smartest. The boys would be in their very best attire, with hair neatly slicked down in place; the dazzling white dresses of the girls evoked "oohs" and "aahs" from the bystanders.

The sun was warm, the walk was long, but nevertheless we sang heartily a favorite chorus of the time:

You and me and them over there
Are all God's family.

A small boy, singing with the same gusto as the rest of us, suddenly espied among the bystanders a lad with whom he must previously have had a disagreement. Quick as lightning, he left the parade, gave chase, and landed a few well-aimed punches on his "friend." Before you could say "Hey, don't you dare do that!" he was back in his place on the march, continuing to sing as earnestly as before:

You and me and them over there
Are all God's family.......

—*Vera Turner*

In the small corps of Caterham, Surrey, southeast London, two small brothers named Stephen and Michael were lively members of the Sunday school. Stephen decided to serve Jesus and become a junior soldier. But young Michael was "a real handful."

One Sunday, shortly after his enrollment, Stephen volunteered to line out the song, "Be strong in the grace of the Lord." As soon as he began, his small brother began to mimic him, "taking the mickey." The reading became:

Be strong in the grace of the Lord...shut yer gob!...
Be noble and upright and true...

—*Doris Martin*

On return from the office, I slumped into an easy chair. My ever-thoughtful wife inquired, "What sort of a day have you had?" I replied, "Oh, I've had a lot of board meetings."

Without even raising her head from the book she was reading, our young daughter murmured, "I've been to a lot of bored meetings, too." To myself I grunted, "Out of the mouths of babes..."

When our daughter was born, our son was ten years old. He had set his heart on having a baby brother with whom he could play. But then he came to terms with the fact of having a sister and wanted to see her as soon as possible after her birth.

Alas, the hospital in which my wife had given birth had a rule which forbade visitors other than the father on the first day. My son was outraged. Looking at me with all the scorn he could command, he said, "But you are only a relation by marriage. I'm a blood relation."

To that logic, I had no reply.

—*Wesley Harris*

Wanting to illustrate the point that sometimes we can answer our own prayers, William Booth, Founder of The Salvation Army, told of a little girl who worried herself into a fearful state of agitation about the birds that became caught in the traps set for them by her brother.

One evening, at her mother's knee, she prayed about her problem. "O Lord, don't let the little birds get into Robbie's traps. Please don't let them." And then, to her mother's astonishment, she added exultantly, "I know they won't, I know they won't, they can't. Amen."

"But, Dolly," remonstrated her mother, "what makes you so sure God will answer your prayers for the birds?" Dolly confidently exclaimed, " 'Cos before I prayed, I went out into the garden and kicked the traps to bits."

—*John Mowat, quoting an article by Lt.-Colonel Arthur Bristow in* The Musician.

When my husband and I were appointed to the command of Los Angeles Tabernacle Corps, it was announced that the congregation would be invited to hold "a pounding" for us after the Sunday evening service. Our two sons, ages 6 and 9, were typical, bursting-with-curiosity little boys. Before the evening service started, they ran around examining the entire suite of buildings, including the kitchen.

They came running to me afterwards with quite frightened looks on their faces. "Mommy, are the people going to pound us with all those sacks of sugar, flour and cans of food?"

—*Judy Watt*

Major Mary Petrov was an inspiring teacher to her class of Sunday school children at a corps in the USA Central Territory. From her adventurous service in so many places, she had a wealth of stories to tell. She was the ideal role model. One girl confided to her mother that when she grew up, she would like to be a Major like Miss Petrov. What would she have to do? she asked.

Her mother tried to explain all that would be involved. It would take quite a long time. First she would have to be a corps cadet, study hard, do her lessons, attend classes. Then, she would need to become a candidate for officership, do more studies, pass an examination board, go to a training college for two years, and then serve as an officer for twenty years before reaching the rank of major, going anywhere in the world where the Army appointed her.

"Oh," said her daughter, "I think I'll be a clown instead."

At Harlow, Essex, we had arranged for Father Christmas to call at the corps with big empty sacks three weeks before Christmas. The idea was that the Sunday school children could fill them with toys and gifts for the less fortunate boys and girls in the town. We had persuaded one member of the congregation to play the role of Santa. So appealing was the idea, it seemed that everyone, young and old, contributed during the gift service, including the four-year-old son of Father Christmas.

When he presented his gift, the boy looked long and hard

at the bewhiskered old gentleman, and walked off the platform deep in thought.

He said nothing more until the family was seated around the dinner table at home. Suddenly, he announced "I think that Father Christmas is a nice man."

His parents looked at him, wondering what was still to come.

The little lad added, "He looks just like my daddy."

—*Arthur J. Brown*

ANN SEAVERS REMEMBERS: Dusty, age six, had a gift for describing exactly what he saw and never doubting that the words used by grown-ups meant exactly what they said. I had left some articles for a bridal shower on the bed.

"Aunty Anne, who are these things for?" he asked, standing with a frying pan in one hand and a lifter in the other. "They are for one of the girls at the corps for her shower," I answered.

"Oh! Like this?" he asked again, placing the frying pan on his head. "To keep her hair from getting wet in the shower?"

Jeff's grandmother had passed away. We explained to the little boy, "Grandma has gone to heaven to be with Jesus."

"Wow!" said Jeff, pointing heavenward. "She sure must have had an awfully long ladder to get way up there."

—*Ann Seavers*

Cappy (the Captain) was passing out toys to her five-year-olds as they arrived at 7 a.m. at the day nursery in Baltimore, Maryland. As Ronnie accepted his puzzle, he sneezed and Cappy said, "God bless you, Ronnie." She went on greeting the other children as they came in.

Suddenly, she heard Ronnie crying and asked him what was the matter.

Looking at her through his tears, he told her: "Cappy, I've got 'God bless you' all over my puzzle."

Such was one of the lighter moments Brigadier Catherine Pinnix remembers from her loving service in the women's social work.

—*Ivy Waterworth*

CHAPTER 11

MANY HAVE FALLEN
BY THE TONGUE

BOTH BIBLE AND APOCRYPHA GIVE SOLEMN warnings about the need to control the tongue. New Testament writer James gets particularly excited about the damage that can be caused by what he describes as "this little member." He acknowledges that there are many ways in which we may all at times slip up. But if a person never slips up in his or her speech, James declares them perfect, able to keep the whole body in check.

However, James is on the track of those with a double tongue or a malicious tongue. He is not writing about the slip-ups sent me by those who "nearly died when the speaker said…" (Should that read "slips-up"? Am I guilty of the first of many "slips -up"?)

Corps Sergeant Majors, those faithful ladies and gentlemen whose task it is to announce in every service the forthcoming events at a Salvation Army corps, are inevitably specially prone to the slip up because they must perform so often. I am assured that Sergeant Major Jack Thompson, of Wallsend, would regularly announce: "If on Monday afternoons, ladies, you have nothing on, the Home League will be very glad to see you." Shouldn't someone have tactfully told him of his error rather than let him blunder on? Or did they enjoy the announcements interlude all the more?

Other announcements I've heard about include: "The person responsible for providing the flowers next Sunday is hanging on the notice board in the foyer"…"It is great to see such a dense crowd here this morning"…."Next week our 11 a.m. holiness meeting will commence at 10:45."

Those who know Major Jorge Booth, of international fame, will wonder if it really was a slip of the tongue when at Plymouth he announced, "Next week, Colonel Hilda Pidgeon will pay us a flying visit."

Their frequency on the public platform makes some Sergeant Majors develop quite a style. Colonel Will Fenwick, a beloved Field Secretary in Britain, recalls as a Captain stationed at Abingdon becoming a good friend of Captain Harold Wright, stationed at the nearby little market town of Chipping Norton. When Harold married and went away on honeymoon, Will agreed to conduct the Sunday services for him at Chipping Norton.

The Corps Sergeant Major there was called Buggins (no kidding!) and delivered the announcements in the kind of country-yokel accent beloved of stage comedians. "Now next Saturday," he began in slow ponderous tones, "we 'ave a meetin' to welcome 'ome the Cap'n and his woife—'cause they've just got married, see! Now we've got some tickets. On the tickets it says 'Stonesfield Band.' but it ain't Stonesfield Band. It's a tea. And it says, 'Admission three pence.' But it ain't three pence, it's noine pence. And the toime ain't sev'n p.m.. It's four-thirrty p.m.."

Maybe wise old Sergeant Major Buggins knew more than most about the art of effective communication!

~~

Salvation Army Trade Departments the world over get

plenty of stick for their alleged short-comings and are seldom without complaints or without stories of customers' howlers, like that of the customer who asked, "May I try on that dress in the window?" or the one who wrote, "Please send me one soft Captain's cap." One complainer wrote: "'My patience is running out over my uniform." Wally Horwood, who worked at the London Trade Headquarters and now, appropriately enough, edits the magazine *Winds,* tells me about the time a goods chute was installed in the packing department. He vividly remembers the query being shouted up the chute, "When are Major Smith's trousers coming down?" Major Iris Port assures me that for some years a visitors' calling card produced by London's Trade Department for the use of corps officers read: "Dear Friend, Today I called and found you out…" No wonder so many fled the country!

A task to challenge the most willing brass instrument repairer faced the London Trade Department when they received a flat piece of metal from Southern Africa. A note explained it had been a cornet, but an elephant had trod on it during an open-air meeting. Could it be repaired, please? (There was no explanation as to why the elephant had been invited to the open-air meeting. Could it have been the singing of "Your tusk is calling you and mine is calling me" that attracted him?)

It seems that Army trade departments around the world are not without their problems. I'm told the staff of the Melbourne Trade Department had a ready answer when a Scotsman walked in and inquired if they had any braid. "You'll be needing a baker's shop, sir," they told him.

～

WAR DAYS IN BRITAIN produced their own crop of howlers and the very amateur, home-grown film section then operating at International Headquarters could be relied on to create havoc out of the simplest camera work. The Brigadier (no less!) in charge resolved to record shots of the relief work being done by women cadets at the International Training

College for people made homeless by bombing. The first sequence was to show a cadet hurrying into the Assembly Hall, obsequiously interrupting a prayer and worship service, and handing a message to Captain Miriam Richards. The Captain was then to announce: "A bomb has dropped on Dog Kennel Hill." (If a bomb had dropped on nearby Dog Kennel Hill, the cadets would have been picking themselves up off the floor and thanking God for his sparing mercies!) "Will emergency team members please go to your stations." With speed but still with the dignity appropriate to the International Training College, the said relief workers would then hurry away.

The sequence was rehearsed several times. Then came the actual "take." "Cut," shouted the Brigadier. The camera wasn't working. "Take 2" began. "Cut," shouted the Brigadier. The lighting was faulty. "Take 3" began. "Cut" shouted the Brigadier. The messenger had tripped climbing the Assembly Hall platform steps. Several more times something went wrong, but patiently Miriam Richards continued to declare, "A bomb has dropped on Dog Kennel Hill."

Finally, everything seemed in order. The Brigadier was sure this time all would be fine. Miriam took the note from the messenger and read with great clarity, "A DOG has dropped on Bomb Kennel Hill."

Mistakes during the wartime blackout were inevitable. Despite the darkness, Lieut.-Colonel Theo Kitching conscientiously resolved that he must complete collecting funds in the district allotted him for the Army's annual appeal. With some relief, he knocked on the door of the very last house in his road. The lady householder opened it and, thinking it was her husband, cried happily, "My beautiful boy, come in!"

〜

A LITTLE KNOWLEDGE CAN SURELY BE a dangerous thing, especially when grappling with a language that is not one's own. Major James Hood, a USA officer who served with his doctor-wife Sallyann in the Army's Catherine Booth Hospital, India, tells of the day International Headquarters wanted passport-size photographs of all missionary officers. The Indian territorial commander dictated a letter to his English secretary for the missionaries, telling them what was needed: *"Please send us a photograph of your bust. It need not be large, but it must be clear and distinct."* Tactfully, hesitantly, respectfully, the English secretary tried to explain that the wording needed to be changed. "You see, sir, some of the ladies...well, they would wonder...actually, they might...O, just take my word for it, let me change it."

A Sunday evening service in English was a regular feature at the Catherine Booth Hospital (CBH). It helped to improve the nursing students' command of English and also ministered to those who could not speak Tamil. When one of the nursing sisters was leaving the hospital for an improved position elsewhere, she asked if she might speak during the service. Very movingly, she told of the impact made by the hospital on her life and how much she had grown spiritually and in character. But, Major Hood confesses, "Some of us did have difficulty maintaining our composure when she declared she had been 'watered, pruned and manured' while at CBH."

~

HOW DULL LIFE WOULD BE if no speaker or writer ever goofed! How rich are those moments, particularly on supposed solemn occasions, when the distinguished visitor says what he did not intend to say! Then for some of us whose giggle-meter reaches boiling point more quickly than that of others, there is the agonizing ecstasy of almost choking with suppressed mirth, of stuffing handkerchief into mouth and trying hard to think of something dismal, lugubrious and glum. For me, a mental picture of London's St. Pancras Railway Station usually restores my gravity.

A Divisional Commander's wife was being shown the respectful attention wise officers usually accord a Divisional Commander's wife during officers' councils, until she said, "The other day I found an old *Local Officer* in the cupboard."

135

Major Iris Port tells me that even those present who knew she was referring to a long-discontinued Army journal joined in the resulting mirth.

The ladies attending a Home League rally in a USA division were somewhat perplexed when, in a sudden explosion of enthusiasm, the Divisional Commander's wife exclaimed at the conclusion of an exciting day, "And now, let us all go forward, stern to stern." Well, it was certainly a change from "hand in hand"!

The 450 ladies who arrived at beautiful Camp Wonderland outside Chicago for a USA Central Territory Home League institute were feeling relaxed and in outgoing mood in the opening meeting after having eaten an excellent dinner. The organizers had persuaded the Territorial Commander, Commissioner Claude E. Bates, to be present at least for the commencement and "say a few words"—an awesome task at any time, but especially for a mere male confronted by 450 light-hearted, animated ladies. Not having anything in particular he wanted to say, the Commissioner decided that he, too, should adopt a relaxed, informal style.

"Did you enjoy your bus ride here?" he bellowed.

"Yeeeeeessss," they chorused back.

"Did you like that first great meal?"

"Yeeeeeessss," they boomed at him.

"Isn't this a marvelous camp?"

"Yeeeeeessss," they yelled.

"And are you all expecting?"

Before he could add anything more, the roar in reply was thunderous and unanimous: "NNNNOOOOOOOO!"

—～—

Lieut.-Colonel Bertie Rolls was renowned as a lovable and loving chubby-cheeked Divisional Commander in the UK, as harmless and guileless as his name suggested. He would often tell about his humble origins and always pay tribute to his hardworking, adorable mother. The large family grew up in the Buckinghamshire town of High Wycombe, noted for its production of furniture. In those days, families would help make chairs at home to scrape together a livelihood, threading and weaving cane to make the seats on wooden chair frames provided by the manufacturers.

"My dear mother," Bertie told his officers gathered in conference, "had to cane ten bottoms every day to make ends meet."

From the back of the room, a witty officer called out above the uproar, "They should have called High Wycombe 'High Whack-em,' Colonel!"

Maybe it wasn't a slip when in the days before fax machines, a USA Divisional Commander sent a two word telegram to one of his officers. It read "Congratulations Stop." Commissioner Robert Thompson tells me the officer's wife had just given birth to their twelfth child. The good Commissioner also tells me he saw the copy of a letter which greeted the recipient as "My Drear Colonel." Was it of any significance, he wonders, that it was addressed to a Chief Secretary?

Corps officers like to receive their divisional boss with every courtesy. When Divisional Commander and Mrs. Milton Anderson led the Sunday meetings at Kenosha Corps, USA Central Territory, Lieutenant and Mrs. Eugene Anderson invited them to their home for lunch. With them was Cadet Robert Bonesteel, who was receiving further training at the corps.

Wanting to encourage the cadet, Lieutenant Anderson explained how Robert had introduced them to a new book of table graces. They had found it very helpful and he was sure the reading indicated for the day would prove appropriate. Without checking what was printed, he began to read:

"When you give a luncheon or dinner party, don't invite your friends or your brothers or your relations or wealthy neighbors, for the chances are they will invite you back and you will be fully repaid. No, when you give a party, invite the poor, the lame, the crippled and the blind. That way lies real happiness for you." (Luke 14:12,13. J.B. Phillips.)

~

Sometimes, it's the solemnity of an occasion, and a meeting leader's over-eagerness to help his congregation realize its significance, that produce a flow of words which won't stand close examination. As Commanding Officer of Annfield Plain Corps, County Durham, northern England, Captain Bernard Smith wanted someone special to conduct services in which several items, including a new corps flag, were to be dedicated to God's service. Lt.-Colonel Herbert Page, the public relations officer from Newcastle, agreed to be his man.

The day was going well. The sacred moment for the new flag to be dedicated came in the afternoon. The Colonel ably spelt out what the tricolor emblem stood for. He described the physical persecution suffered by some Salvationists in defending the flag in street meetings during the movement's early days. Then came the prayer of dedication. With utmost gravity, the Colonel invited the congregation "to bow your heads, close your eyes, and look at the flag." Bernard admits he found it difficult to be reverent at that moment. And he didn't have the heart to tell the Colonel afterward what he had said.

It may have been over-eagerness to tell a farewelling young officer how much he was liked that caused a Home League member to tell him in a farewell speech: *"It's we old ladies who will miss you most. We have always felt you were one of us."*

~

AS MENTIONED EARLIER, the freedom offered the lay person to "speak, sing or pray" in meetings is a tradition carefully cherished in The Salvation Army. Not often is it abused, though—as Captain Beverly Ivany reminds me—some people love to hear themselves "wax eloquent," even in public prayer. She writes:

"I recall as a child (and even in recent years) cringing

when certain people rose to pray, knowing they'd go on and on, often insensitive to worship. At a particular meeting, prayer was requested for the work of the League of Mercy (comprising compassionate people giving both practical and spiritual help to the ill and elderly). 'Would anyone like to offer prayer on behalf of this special outreach?' The man stood. Round the world he went, praying for everyone and everything. His voice rose high to the mountain top, then lowered to a whisper. It was hard to focus on the sincerity of his prayer.

"Finally, after what seemed like two hours (probably eight minutes), he recalled what he was supposed to be praying for. In his fluctuating yet booming voice, he blurted out: *'Please, please, bless the League of Wercy Merkers. AMEN'."*

Sometimes a lack of understanding can clothe an old word in exciting new colors, as a Canadian retired officer recalls when she and her husband were at Stephenville, Newfoundland, leading Sunday meetings. "A light came out of darkness" was being sung in the morning holiness meeting, to the swinging accompaniment of band and the beat of drums. "We were well into the second verse," she recalls, "when I noticed one of the young timbrelists hesitate over a word in the fifth line: 'He *wooed* and won them to him, by love...' She had obviously never seen the word before and had no idea as to its meaning. But nothing daunted, with jubilant voice she sang loud and clear, 'He *wowed* and won them to Him, by love...' As the significance of the word she had used took hold of me, I could have shouted 'Bravo' or maybe 'Glory' would have been more appropriate for a holiness meeting. But in that moment of revelation, I knew the little girl was singing more truly than she realized."

From a long and distinguished career in Canada, Lieut.-Colonel Bob Chapman remembers several occasions when his composure was tested by some sincere soul's unusual phrase. For instance, there was the Corps Sergeant Major of a small western corps who was so thankful for the stream of newcomers being attracted to the Sunday meetings. Invariably in the Tuesday night prayer meeting, she would thank the Lord "for the many strange faces coming to our meetings." In the same corps was a lady who for years had not had the advantage of indoor plumbing. With excitement in her voice she told the corps officer, "Captain, do you know that very soon I will be getting the *fatalities* in my house?"

Then there was the young convert, limited in education, who in an Easter Sunday morning testimony during a street meeting declaimed, "I sure am glad he *arised*." Another dear sister assured her listeners that "God is no *respectable* person."

In earlier days, recalls the Colonel, the proverbial prayer offered by local officers before the Sunday night salvation meeting was for the Lord to go "from heart to heart and from seat to seat." Also testing the imagination were the familiar prayers, "Lord, bless the sick of our corps," "Bless those on beds of pain" or sometimes in street meetings "Bless those who are sick behind the curtains" and "Bless those laid on one side." Such imagery causes the mind to boggle and the uninitiated to giggle.

$$\sim$$

Commissioner Ed. Carey remembers an officer who shrank from public work being asked to read from Scripture about the calling of the twelve apostles. Matthew 10:2 came out as, "Now the names of the twelve *impossibles* are these:" Maybe more truth than just a rhyming slip, suggests the Commissioner!

Commissioner Wesley Harris recalls visiting a provincial city in Australia where the local mayor introduced him as "The Chief Executor of The Salvation Army." The Commissioner adds, "Mercifully, although I have been an Army executive, I have not been called on to read its last will and testament."

Good friends of the Army often admit to having held mistaken views when they come to examine the movement more closely. Mrs. Colonel Emily Fritz tells me of an orientation class her husband, as Major Ed Fritz, held for prospective advisory board members in White Plains, N.Y. After Ed explained the meaning of the Army's flag, one of the men confessed, "I'm surprised to learn that the words on the flag are 'Blood and Fire.' Because of all the disaster work you do, I thought the words were 'Flood and Fire'."

The slip of the pen or typewriter can have more long-term consequences than the mere slip of the tongue, as Lt.-Colonel Howard R. Evans related at his retirement luncheon concerning days when he was Divisional Secretary in Pennsylvania. As such, he sent proposals for a new corps building in Wilmington, Delaware, to the Territorial Property Secretary. The plans called for the new structure to be built around a small courtyard and to include a flagpole on which the Army's tricolor emblem and the stars and stripes would be displayed.

Word came back from the Property Secretary that the board wanted to have the flagpole illuminated. Conscientiously, Lt.- Colonel Evans requested the architect to re-draw the plans to include flagpole floodlighting.

Back went the project to territorial headquarters. A somewhat apologetic Property Secretary replied. His secretary had misunderstood his original dictation. The Property Board did not want the flagpole illuminated. They wanted it *eliminated*.

Considerable publicity awaits the poster-writer or notice-board artist who goofs. The *Reader's Digest,* no less, got hold of one ardent evangelist's unintended fiery warning, so Major Stanley Richardson tells me. The colorful poster on the large notice board outside a Salvation Army citadel showed traffic lights set at red. The caption warned: "STOP! ARE YOU ON YOUR WAY TO HELL?" Underneath was the permanent gold-letter wording that regularly coaxed passers-by: "A warm welcome awaits you inside."

Brigadier John Thomson has a somewhat similar story about an officer friend of his in Glasgow, Scotland. Having been a sign writer by profession before becoming an officer, he always enjoyed exercising his skill by announcing the theme of his Sunday services on the notice board. One week it read:

> 11 a.m. Holiness unto the Lord
> 6.30 p.m. What will it be like in hell?
> *Come and hear our band in the shopping*
> *centre on Saturday morning at 10 a.m.*

Surely one has to commend such honesty!

To conclude this chapter on "slip-ups" I go back again to that good New Testament writer James and his solemn warning about the dangers of the wagging tongue. For James surely has a modern day disciple in the good and gifted Colonel Rowland D. Hughes, the previously mentioned former Editor-in-Chief in New York. The always mirthful Rowland writes scathingly about the double-talk that he would like to see eradicated not only from the current media but also from Salvation Army platforms and pronouncements, too.

He's in his most fluent stride here:

BIG-DOMED EDUCATORS TALK of "Subschool interest groups" to cover up the fact that students are learning to sew, dance or play basketball instead of to read and write. Children are not lazy any more; they're "under-achievers." And please don't call today's kids stupid; they're "slow learners." They're not anti-social either; they have only "inadequate relationship to peer group," says the report card. Nor are they ineducable; they are "unable to benefit meaningfully from classroom dynamics."

Charismatic, ecumenicity, multimedia, conceptualization—these and such other fancy-pants words I have heard tossed around our platforms by officers with more degrees than a thermometer (and who ought to know better) as well as by some of the veriest dumb-bells who just made it out of the training school by the skin of their bridgework. It's all "baffletalk" which unfailingly sends their hearers into lethargy and straight into the lap of Morpheus.

And let's not forget the Army's "officialese." Let me translate just a smidgen of it for all you dear souls to whom it is all Greek:

"In-depth reassessment." ("We kicked it around at lunch.")

"Note and initial." ("Let's share the responsibility for this.")

"A survey is being made." ("We need more time on this one—a lot more time!")

"A committee is now being appointed." ("The suggestion is as good as dead right now.")

"We're holding this in abeyance." ("Forget it! We don't intend to disturb the status quo.")

"Your idea has stimulated discussion, provoked thought and opened new vistas." ("What nut sent this one in?")

BUT IF EVER WE OUGHT TO SAY WHAT WE MEAN, if ever we ought to avoid "out of town language," then it is when we are trying to explain the wonder of the Christian gospel message. Yet what do we hear?

Witnessing to their faith on a busy street corner, with all the fire and faith that can be mustered, many who wear the blue serge uniform of a Salvationist speak of "a fountain opened to the House of David," "a balm in Gilead," "a born-again Christian," "a brand plucked from the burning," "salvation through grace," "justification through faith," "feasting on the milk, the honey and the wine," "dwelling in Beulah Land" and "sweeping through the gates of the New Jerusalem." No question about it, these folk are sincere, genuinely concerned, and motivated by an all-consuming desire to let men and women in on the good news that Christ meets the deepest needs of the human heart.

But, unfortunately for the dear folk standing round—so many of whom have never been to church, looked inside a

Bible or read a religious publication—the message of the well-intentioned Salvationists is utterly meaningless. If we expect to open minds and hearts to the music and magic of the gospel, many of us will have to learn how to communicate. And in a tall hurry! Otherwise, unlike Jesus who spoke of the simple, the ordinary and the familiar—birds, sheep, lilies, trees, seeds, bread—and whom the common people heard gladly, we'll be off in a corner somewhere, talking to ourselves.

St. Paul brings it all into focus: "Except ye utter by the tongue words easy to be understood, how shall it be known what is spoken? For ye shall speak into the air." (I Corinthians 14:9)

CHAPTER 12

EMBARRASSING MOMENTS

YEARS AGO, A POPULAR PERSONALITY heard regularly on the British Broadcasting network was a jovial Yorkshireman named Wilfred Pickles. With such a surname, he had a head start over his fellow commentators and reporters.

In a long-running radio series, he visited villages, towns and cities across the length and breadth of the British Isles. People packed the theaters and community halls where he staged his simple yet compellingly attractive programs: a format of community singing and personal interviews. People chosen to interview were just ordinary citizens, known to no one but their friends, work mates and neighbors. No big names. No personalities of stage and screen. With gentle skill, courtesy and warm friendliness, he coaxed them to tell about their lives and give their opinions. He demonstrated the well-known fact that behind everyone there is a fascinating story waiting to be told.

Each interview would include one riveting question. In

his broad accent, he would ask "Have you ever had an embarrassing moment?" Invariably, he was told of such a moment.

Working on the frontiers of raw human need and interfacing constantly with people both in private and in public meetings, most Salvationists would admit to having had an embarrassing moment—or two! By no means all are self-inflicted. What growing son or daughter has not found how embarrassing parents can be?

I was eleven years old when my mum and dad decided I should accompany them to London to see eldest brother Wycliffe commissioned after having completed his cadet training. The demands of conducting three indoor services and three street meetings on Sunday in the down-at-heel part of Manchester where my parents ministered meant we must catch the "red-eye special," leaving the railway station at 11:45 p.m. The reduction in fare for such an overnight run also suited father's ever impecunious condition.

My first impression of the big city, outside Euston Station at 6 a.m., was discouraging. In my short-trousered young people's band member uniform, I shivered with cold and sleepiness. I was hungry, too. Surely there was a restaurant open somewhere. There was, but father had read in *The War Cry* that the Trade Headquarters in Judd Street would open at 7 a.m. to serve breakfasts. "We'll walk around and see some of the great sights until seven o'clock." (I began to understand why my other brother and sister thought father was "Army-barmy.") I noted the absence of any great sights.

The morning passed in a blur of trying to find our way around. Somehow we reached Kensington for the afternoon commissioning ceremony in the Royal Albert Hall. Its vastness awed me. Across its spaciousness I peered, seeking to identify big brother on stage. Then I spotted him as it was his turn to be appointed. Father and Mother were in a tizzy, straining to see and to hear. "Cadet Wycliffe Pratt, you are appointed a sergeant to the International Training College," announced Commissioner Samuel Hurren, the Training Principal.

Father could not restrain his joy and pride at what he felt to be the highest accolade heaven could bestow upon his eldest child. There in the arena before 5,000 spectators (most of whom, thankfully, could not possibly see or hear him) he leapt to his feet and called aloud, "WELL DONE, MY BOY!" I blushed in the semi-darkness of the stage-lighted hall. Even eleven-year-olds have their feelings.

We were back again in the evening for the newly commissioned officers' pageant. The opening stirring martial hymn was followed by quiet prayer. Father knelt, as he always did for prayer, his head cradled in his arm resting on the seat in front of him. When the "Amen" was said, father continued to kneel in prayer. Clearly, father was seeking yet extra blessing on what had been for him a spiritually uplifting day. Then came a clash of cymbals and an opening fanfare from the staff band. Dad started, gave a low snort, glanced around in much amazement and slid self-consciously back on to his seat. Those three outdoor and indoors meetings, plus the "red-eyed special" journey, had gotten the better of him. For the second-time that day, I blushed for father.

Eleven years later, I was a cadet in the officer training college myself, hurrying back across the Mediterranean from three years wartime service with the Royal Navy. Even so, I arrived six weeks after the session had commenced and found myself in the dining hall seated at a table where other late arrivals were gathered.

As mentioned earlier, the training session totaled 97 men and 220 women cadets, a residue of six years of war when no male cadets could be admitted. Almost all the men had been in the Forces. Only a few weeks before arriving at the college, they had been exploding depth charges at enemy submarines, launching torpedoes, flying the new jet fighters screaming over hostile territory. Some were veterans of the North Africa and Italy campaigns, others of the invasion across Europe. A few were recently released prisoners-of-war. Now, we must sit at desks studying "Orders and Regulations for Home Leagues" and prepare for spiritual warfare!

The cease-fire had not brought an end to clothes or food rationing. Within the college we wore our service uniforms and took our meager weekly rations of butter and sugar with us to the dining hall. They never lasted more than two or three days.

One breakfast time, I suggested to a newly arrived fellow cadet that he put salt on his porridge oats as the Scots do instead of sugar, since he had none. We were in fairly hilarious mood, as always, and he tried it. He gulped down a mouthful and grinning all over his face declared, *"It tastes no bloody different!"*

Unaccustomed to such adjectives, the walls of the hallowed institution might well have collapsed. They didn't. More importantly, none of us at the table collapsed. We were neither embarrassed nor shocked. We simply fell apart with laughter. For we understood. We, too, had just emerged from years saturated by mess-deck language of crude vulgarity and blasphemy. By comparison, his word paled into insignificance. But the cadet himself was embarrassed. He asked to see the Chief Side Officer and express his feeling that he needed more time to adjust. Sadly, we did not hear of the lad again.

HOW YOU HANDLE A POTENTIALLY embarrassing moment is, of course, an indicator of your skill and probably your experience. For me, one experience as a member of *The War Cry* staff, reporting a farewell meeting of General Albert Orsborn at Tunbridge Wells just prior to his retirement, remains unforgettable. He had preached with his customary powerful, faultless, note-free oratory and persuasion. Now he was inviting any in the crowded auditorium who wanted to accept Christ as Lord of their lives to move quietly forward to the altar. One could almost feel the tension of the tussle taking place in people's minds and hearts.

Suddenly a baby's cry rang out, shattering the atmosphere—so I thought. But, no! Betraying no hint of irritation, the remarkable leader quietly commented, *"Just as that baby's cry rings out through this auditorium, so let your cry go up to Almighty God. And just as this mother seeks to comfort her little one, so will a Father God seek to comfort you."*

Magnificent! A brilliant example of taking captivity captive and so effective in saving a mother from any embarrassment on such a public occasion. It was an object lesson to an impressionable young Captain!

That I needed such lessons was evident from a Sunday evening service at Caterham, south London, where fellow Cadet Sergeant Bramwell Davies and I conducted the meeting. As I preached, I leaned for emphasis on the outer end of the reading desk. It snapped, banged its way to the altar amid gasps of shock from the elderly congregation, and left me spread-eagled, bent double over the rostrum. No wise Orsborn-like words came to me as I struggled back to an upright stance. Unable to speak, the laughter-ridden Bram Davies could only nod his head in agreement when I suggested it was time to pronounce the benediction.

I did somewhat better at the commencement of British Congress meetings being held in 1972 in the Empire Pool, Wembley. I had persuaded Mr. Jack Warner, famous as the typical British "copper" in the television police station series, "Dixon of Dock Green," to be star guest of honor at the opening outdoor concert by the Army's headline-hitting "Joy Strings" pop group.

Sitting beside him on the high stage, I became aware of an officer behind and below me trying to attract my attention. I got the message: our distinguished guest's trouser zip was undone. I leaned over Jack, ostensibly to point out something on the large program which now covered him, and whispered, "You need to do up your zip, Jack." He grinned, thanked me, and all went well. No need for his famous slogan, " 'Ello, 'ello, what's all this then?"

The timing of the moment of embarrassment can play a major part in deciding whether the situation is retrievable or not. It wasn't for Major Stan Ratcliffe, when as Asst. Public

Relations Secretary on Canada's Territorial Headquarters, he organized the annual Red Shield appeal launch at Hamilton, Ontario. He had succeeded in attracting a packed-out attendance of paying influential guests to the hotel luncheon. There was a top-table of VIPs on the stage, at the end of which he seated himself. All went well, including his own address setting out goals and needs. Then to conclude, the Advisory Board Chairman called on successful Stan to come again to the microphone and pronounce the benediction.

Throughout the lunch, Stan had realized his chair was precariously close to the end of the raised platform. Perhaps it was relief that this important event was just about over that made him forget just how close. But as he pushed back his chair it went over the edge, taking him with it. Rather flustered, he picked himself up off the floor and hurried to the mike. He began his prepared prayer:

"Now unto Him that is able to keep you from falling, and to present you faultless..." The remainder of the benediction was lost in gales of laughter.

Some embarrassing moments become public only when the culprit (or the culprit's spouse) is decent enough to tell about the incident. Members of the Editorial and Literary Department in days gone by enjoyed the account Lieut.-Colonel John Atkinson gave of his wife's other-worldly naiveté. She had agreed to baby-sit their two-year-old grandson, but soon found the task of entertaining the child quite a strain. She turned for help to the television and was glad to see listed in the "Radio Times" that a program called "Racing for Two-year-olds" was just commencing. Ideal, she thought to herself. Only after the child had been watching for half-an-hour did she realize she was introducing her innocent little one to the intrigues of horse-racing and gambling.

~

But I've promised anonymity to the young woman officer, serving on headquarters in the UK, who agreed to lead Sunday meetings at Bognor Regis on Britain's south coast. She was always most careful about her appearance. In particular, in Army uniform one would have to say her appearance was immaculate. Although she preferred a short hair style, she would wear a false bun with her bonnet, recognizing that the Army's traditional headgear really demanded a bun. Few who did not know her would have detected the hair piece.

Just as the evening meeting was about to commence, she was advised that a titled lady was in the congregation. Although a distinguished person, the lady was rather eccentric and given to calling out a comment on anything being done or said. The headquarters Captain was grateful for the advice.

The meeting proceeded smoothly. The titled lady's conduct could not be faulted. With relief, the Captain gave her final prayer and benediction. But scarcely had she said the "Amen" when the lady broke her silence. "Now go home and take off that ridiculous bun," she instructed.

~

ENOUGH OF MY RECOLLECTIONS! I'm indebted to a host of my friends for the following descriptions of times when there were moments of embarrassment. First, but not for the first time in this collection of anecdotes, I present Captain Beverly Ivany.

A FINE BODY

The congress meetings were going extremely well. Everyone enjoyed the fervent singing, the clapping, the praise, the joy that was so evident. The building was packed. The songs were lively, exuberant.

Suddenly, heads turned and people started pointing. Everyone strained to see what all the commotion was about. Then they saw for themselves. Down one of the main aisles came a young man running—with no clothes on! Ushers came out of the woodwork, hurrying to try to cover various parts of his body with their brochures.

The Commissioner's wife stepped to the microphone.

"What a beautiful body! What a fine body God has given to this young man! Let us give God praise!"

An unusual response perhaps. But what else does one say in such circumstances?

WHO'S THAT KNOCKING?

We were into the prayer meeting. Would anyone come forward to kneel at the altar? Surely someone would. The message of a Christ who stands patiently knocking at our heart's closed door had been faithfully delivered. Several choruses of appeal had been sung. Prayer had been offered. The officer suggested that someone else might wish to pray or perhaps to strike up an appropriate chorus.

And very earnestly a dear lady began quietly to sing,

"Who's that knocking at my door?"

Everyone present picked up on the second and third lines, which they knew instinctively were a repeat of the first line. But when the fourth line was to be uttered by the sincere, sensitive congregation, they realized to their astonishment that it was,

"Cried the fair young maiden."

Everyone hummed along in subdued embarrassment, now also realizing that the "chorus" to the dear lady's chosen "prayer song" was,

"It's only me from over the sea,
Cried Barnacle Bill the sailor."

Needless to say, the "prayer-time" quietly ended as we moved into the last congregational song for the meeting!

~~~

FROM MRS. LT.- COLONEL HAZEL RICE:

During World War II the West coast of the USA was under very strict regulations as a precaution against enemy attack. One of the Los Angeles corps was holding a weeknight meeting with the Major's wife preaching the gospel message, when suddenly the red alert sounded. It meant that every light had to be extinguished immediately.

Mrs. Major hesitated for a moment, but then decided that whatever the circumstances, whether she and the congregation could see or not see, she must be faithful and continue giving the message the Lord had given to her.

Within a few minutes, the all clear sounded and the lights came back on. The hall was empty! While it was dark, the small congregation had quietly folded its tents and slipped away.

FROM THE LATE LT.- COLONEL THEO. KITCHING: (provided by his daughter, JOY)

HOME LEAGUE IN HEAVEN

The bombing of Britain became so regular during the six years of World War II that some individuals actually got used to it and became quite indifferent to the danger. When a small bomb exploded on part of a Salvation Army hall, police cordoned off the entire premises, fearing that an unexploded missile might still be among the wreckage.

A police officer routinely checking the premises found a little old lady seated alone in the hall. "What on earth are you doing here?" exclaimed the astonished policeman. "Don't you know there may be an unexploded bomb beneath you?"

"I'm waiting for the Home League meeting," explained the lady innocently.

"My good woman, if you don't hurry up and get out of here, you may have your next Home League in heaven," cried the officer.

WHITHER BOUND?

Although it caused some laughter, I felt it was somewhat inopportune and indiscreet when an officer (who from time to time carried banners through the streets of London) entered the Salvation Army hall where my bride and I were getting married. He carried a banner bearing the words: "HEAVEN OR HELL—WHITHER BOUND?"

FROM BRIGADIER JOHN THOMPSON:

I was the Commanding Officer of the Salvation Army corps at King's Lynn, England, soon after the end of World War II. The town was still full of German prisoners of war, awaiting repatriation to their homeland. Some of them used to attend our meetings.

One morning I was at the hall, "tinkering" with the organ, when a P.O.W. entered and stood beside me. He showed great interest in my simple playing and now and again commented, "Ver goot." With his own fingers, he seemed to be trying to copy my chord work. So I showed him how to build the chords of "C" and "D" major. I thought I was making some impression on the good man, especially when he indicated he would like to try them for himself. So I slid off the stool.

As he brought his two hands down on the keyboard for a massive fortissimo chord, the Camp Commandant came into the hall. "Ah, Captain," he exclaimed, "thank you for looking after Hans. He was the deputy organist at Stuttgart Cathedral before Hitler called him up."

My face was like unto a beetroot. My Adam's apple worked overtime. My eyes were like chapel hat pegs.

FROM MAJOR ARTHUR J. BROWN:

When the Divisional Youth Secretary was given the opportunity to preach during divisional councils before he farewelled from the Liverpool Division, he chose to speak on the unusual text: "You stay here with the ass while I go yonder" (Genesis 22:5). Its significance was not lost on many hearers. Alas, it was well known that the D.Y.S. disagreed violently and frequently with his Divisional Commander.

I confirm the veracity of this story. I was present in the Kensington hall on the occasion.

FROM HARRY SPARKS, PASADENA, CALIFORNIA:

The Pasadena Corps Sergeant Major, Brigadier Jen Jensen (R), one of God's choice saints, telephoned the commanding officer. When the voice responded with "Hello!" Jensen broke into song. "Sunshine on the hill," he chorused, "there is sunshine on the hill." When he had finished, he jovially inquired, "Well, how did you like that?"

"Fine," said the voice at the other end of the line, "but who are you?"

Only then did the Brigadier realize he had phoned the wrong number. GULP!

FROM ARLEE LANSING, NORTHERN CALIFORNIA:

Our division was holding its Self-Denial appeal ingathering with national pageantry. Several officers were dressed in the national costumes of the countries in which the Army serves. They were being lined up on the platform when CHINA, who was wearing black silk Chinese trousers, lost them! She was unaware of the silky black around her ankles until MEXICO, standing near, whispered audibly in shock, "CHINA, you lost your pants."

One of the songsters, the Home League secretary, seated nearby, whispered, "Home League to the rescue!" The costumed countries closed around CHINA as her trousers were pinned up. All the while, the audience laughed uproariously. The bandsmen (of course!) had difficulty playing for laughter.

Finally peace was restored. That is, until the Divisional Commander made his final, thoughtful remarks intending to close the meeting on a high note of dedication and spirituality.

"Many things have been revealed to us this evening," he declared in all innocence. The audience was off again in hearty laughter.

FROM LT.-COLONEL BERT HILL, CANBERRA, AUSTRALIA:

I was excited at the prospect of Commissioner Edgar Grinsted (Territorial Commander, Australia East) visiting my corps at Mackay, even though his schedule only allowed time for him to address a meeting with the Home League ladies. The detailed arrangements had to be done by myself, for my wife was away from the corps expecting our baby.

It was probably due to the inexperience of a young C.O. that I chose cane chairs for him, the Divisional Commander and myself to sit on. The Commissioner had previously indicated he would be willing to play a piano solo in the meeting, and it was evident from the commencement that he was eager to get on with it. In fact, he was quite restless. Almost before his introduction was completed, he leapt to his feet and bounded forward toward the piano. As he did so, the cane seat caught his trousers.

The loud rip of protesting serge was accompanied by some muffled laughter and cries of "Oh, dear!" from some of the Home Leaguers.

"Ladies," said Commissioner Grinsted, "I am coming down off the platform to play the piano. When I reach the stool I shall turn round and you must all close your eyes for two seconds while I sit down."

The ladies later agreed that their energetic Territorial Commander, a former dashing pilot in World War I Royal Flying Corps, was quite a tearaway.

FROM THE LATE LT.-COLONEL LYELL RADER, D.D., O.F.:

Commissioner Wm. McIntyre, when Provincial Commander for the New England Province, was presiding over a meeting attended by a large crowd and at which a distinguished Bishop had agreed to be the speaker. The good Bishop was in full oratorical flight with his mouth wide open when suddenly his bridge flipped up and he couldn't close his mouth.

McIntyre recognized the problem. He leapt to his feet and lifted off his own toupee, crying aloud, "It's O.K., Bishop. We've all got a few problems at our age."

His prompt action convulsed the crowd but it wonderfully and so thoughtfully distracted attention from the embarrassed Bishop until he could adjust his dentures again.

FROM *SWEEPING THROUGH THE LAND* (page 110) by Colonel Wm.G. Harris:

Commissioner Wm. McIntyre possessed lightning wit. He had been invited to be the guest speaker at a large church gathering. The pastor introduced him in glowing terms and was especially complimentary about his fine head of hair.

McIntyre stood and thanked the pastor for his kind words. Then reaching up and lifting off his toupee, he quipped, "You can get the same head of hair for $25!"

FROM MAJOR CLIFF KENT, UK:

After conducting the Sunday morning meeting at Weymouth Corps, I made my way, as customary, to the back of the hall to shake hands with members of the congregation as they left. Remaining in the hall were three ladies with walking frames, all sitting together.

As I approached them, one said to me, "This is critics' corner, you know."

Half expecting some criticism after such a greeting and wondering if I had upset them in some way, I responded, "So you're critics are you? Nice to meet you. We need people like you, providing your criticism is constructive."

"Who said anything about criticism?" replied the first lady. "I said, 'This is arthritics' corner'."

FROM COLONEL JOHN BATE, USA NATIONAL HEAD-QUARTERS:

When we returned home to New Zealand after our first term in South America, I used to use a Spanish term of endearment to my wife—mi querida—meaning "my loved one." I didn't use it all the time, but there were moments when it seemed appropriate!

My appointment was that of Aide de Camp (ADC) to the Territorial Commander in New Zealand. On one occasion, when we had been away on tour for three weeks, I drove the Commissioner home and from his quarters phoned my wife to say I would be home within 20-30 minutes. Since she was in our kitchen preparing supper, she opened the front door so I could immediately enter on arrival.

She had been back in the kitchen only a few minutes when she heard the familiar cry, "Mi querida, mi querida." With this, she turned and ran through the kitchen and up the hallway, arms outstretched, responding, "Mi querida, mi querida."

The man from the electric light company standing at the front door by the power box had a look of utter surprise on his face.

Finding the door unlocked he had entered, calling out "Meter reader, meter reader." He acknowledged that not all housewives welcomed him with such a warm greeting.

FROM ADVISORY BOARD CHAIRMAN WILLIAM T. WASTE, SAN FRANCISCO:

"WE'RE GOING TO PRAY FOR IT"

Our advisory board was discussing a large and very expensive project and its feasibility. It entailed a great many risks but had a very worthwhile purpose as its goal. But the conclusion of the board was that, regardless of the great benefit that would result, we simply couldn't come up with the financing, given the constituency's prior record. Every sensible and responsible business evaluation, in spite of our love for the Army and the need for the project, just didn't give us any confidence in our ability not only to avoid failing, but even to avoid a real downside disaster.

But it seemed the Army officers were simply not receiving our message. Finally, in desperation, we asked, "Where is the money to come from?"

"We'll pray for it," they answered.

Those of us who were used to dealing with quarterly board meetings of stockholders, notably steely-eyed in their approach to this kind of situation, were undone. We said, "You're going to do what?" They repeated, "We're going to pray for it'."

The meeting rambled on for a short time and then broke up with we "outsiders" considerably troubled.

The next chapter is easy or I wouldn't be telling it. It was decided to go for it, with board members being dragged along "kicking and screaming." AND ULTIMATELY IT WAS A SUCCESS.

We had all prayed long, hard and loud—and apparently were heard. I do not recommend the procedure for all projects, either for The Salvation Army or in the harsh reality of the outside world. It was a marvelous demonstration, however, of faith, determination, hard work, good planning—and PRAYER (and maybe a little luck, who knows?).

The beautiful humor of all this is to realize that in the board's love for the Army and our desire to keep it from trouble, we had failed to look a little further. I have told this story many times and the inherent humor in it still amuses me.

THE MOST DELICIOUS DESSERT

Our division gives an annual civic luncheon each year which is both a fund-raiser and a public relations event. It is a large, prestigious occasion with high-level downtown business and community representation. Attendance is at the 700 range with national personalities represented. My wife and I sponsor a table. We invite interested friends and always have a uniformed officer couple with us to talk about the real work the Army is doing.

On the occasion I'm describing everything was going well. The hotel had gone all-out to produce a first-class, well-served luncheon. The dessert was ice cream with an appealing green and dark-colored swirl of sauce. The lovely and earnest young Lieutenant who was seated to my left tried her dessert first and turned to me ecstatically. "It's the most delicious dessert I've ever had." I smiled and said I must try it.

To my horror I identified the "sauce" as creme de menthe and a coffee liqueur. The luncheon committee, with minds focused primarily on the program, had left the dessert to the chef's discretion. We should have known better and were all apologies. No irreparable harm was done. The Lieutenant was not sent on the road to perdition. But I still smile when I recollect the delight in the eyes of that innocent young lady.

〰️

FROM CAPTAIN JACK L. PHILLIPS, USA WESTERN TERRITORY:

When Lt.-Colonel and Mrs. Frank Moss, as divisional leaders, visited Anna and myself in Farmington, New Mexico, they cheered us with the story of their visit to take lunch at an important advisory board member's home.

All went well up to the moment when dessert was served. It appeared to be tapioca pie. According to Mrs. Moss, her husband was so taken by the delicious taste of this tapioca pie, he "ranted and raved" for at least five minutes about it. He insisted that Ruth must ask for the recipe.

When they had left, Ruth could scarcely wait to ask Frank why he had so "ranted and raved" about the tapioca pie. "Because it was such a delicious tapioca pie," explained Frank.

"But it wasn't tapioca," declared Ruth. "It was a lemon pie not properly prepared, so it was lumpy."

"Why didn't you kick me, or somehow interrupt me?" questioned the now embarrassed Frank.

"But I did kick you, five or six times," protested Ruth.

"No you didn't," said Frank. Obviously she had been kicking their distinguished host.

———

FROM MAJOR STANLEY RICHARDSON, UK:

The women cadets were marching down to Camberwell from the International Training College. I was walking in the opposite direction. Two old ladies were watching the cadets and commenting aloud. As I passed them I heard the following snatch of their conversation:

"Don't they look lovely!"

"Yes, my dear. You'd never believe they'd all been naughty girls, would you!"

———

FROM THE USA SOUTHERN TERRITORY:

Major Stanley Jaynes, while serving as the Divisional Secretary in the Maryland Division, made a long trip out to their furthest corps, Bluefield, West Virginia, to conduct an inspection. He left divisional headquarters after several hours of heavy work, but arriving in Bluefield a little earlier than expected, he decided to work an hour or so with the commanding officer even though he felt very weary.

Prior to beginning the inspection, Major Jaynes bowed his head and began to pray, asking the Lord for guidance and strength, particularly since he was so mentally weary. Indeed, even as he prayed, he sensed he was losing his concentration and heard himself saying, "quote, period, paragraph," as though he were dictating.

When he returned to divisional headquarters, he sportingly told the story on himself. Next day, Captain Bruce Smith, a member of his staff walked up to the Major's office while he was dictating. He immediately apologized and stepped back, saying he didn't want to interrupt him.

"Oh, that's all right," Major Jaynes assured him, "I was only dictating."

"Oh," quipped Captain Bruce, "I thought you were praying, Major."

〰️

FROM CAPTAIN DIANA ZILM, AUSTRALIA:

My husband always took his role as pastor and shepherd very seriously, but it gained a new dimension at one corps. The corps owned a large block of land, part of which was grassed. Keeping it respectably trimmed was a problem. When one of the soldiers suggested we get a couple of sheep to eat the grass, John thought it was a great idea. However, early one Saturday morning he was awakened with the news that his two prize sheep were merrily trotting down the main road of the town in the direction of the big city. After a couple of hours on his motorbike trying to round them up, he brought them home. He was not amused.

From then on he was known in that small country town as the shepherd who lost his flock!

〰️

TWO REPORTS TELL A SIMILAR STORY:

Major Edward Carey was to be the speaker at the Kingston, N.Y. Rotary Club. After lunch, the president of the club turned to him and asked, "Would you like to speak now, or should we let the boys enjoy themselves a little longer?" Report number two says at another Rotary Club where Major Carey was due to speak, the song leader led the club in several rousing numbers. The president then stood to introduce the Major: "Well, we would have liked to enjoy the music a little longer, but unfortunately we have a speaker."

〰️

FROM MAJOR GEORGE WHITTINGHAM, UK:

The North Scotland Division covers a very large area of beautiful but very rugged countryside. It's a challenge for a

Divisional Commander to make sure none of his officers and corps comrades feels left alone and uncared for. One Saturday morning, my wife and I set out from divisional headquarters in Aberdeen to drive to the Lieutenant at the Findochty Corps on the Moray Coast and also look in on the Buckie and Cullen Outpost.

Even though we were in a hurry, we had to drive carefully. Some of the country roads are very narrow. As we turned one corner, an elderly man on a bicycle, not expecting a car to be traveling in his village, swerved over to the curbside and fell off. We stopped and hurried over to him. He assured us he was not hurt and in his warm-hearted Scottish way told us there was no need to be bothered about him. But I insisted he take my calling card and telephone us if in fact he suffered any repercussions.

We didn't hear from him at all. But after the weekend when back at the office, I studied my card for the first time and wondered what our cyclist friend must have thought when he saw the reverse side. It read: "SORRY WE MISSED YOU TODAY."

FROM CAPTAIN PAUL LESLIE, CANADA:

Harold Pye was a trophy of grace. This London-born seaman had drifted from port to port around the world until he wound up on Vancouver's skid row. There, he found the Lord through the Harbor Light ministry.

Harold was one of those simple souls who radiated his joy in knowing Christ and wanted to share that joy with others. He was infatuated with his Army uniform and wore it with pride in many areas of service. Above all, he wanted to be part of a Salvation Army band.

Our corps Bandmaster was sympathetic to Harold's desire and agreed he could become the drummer. Harold's delight knew no bounds. Perhaps it was his awe at gaining the responsibility that made him timid at times. He had to be encouraged to play fortissimo when occasion demanded.

One Sunday evening, the band was on duty for a united service in a small Baptist church. Space was tight for a twenty-piece band playing the chosen selection, "The King's Highway." The concluding section of the theme tune, "We're on the King's Highway," gives the drummer the rare opportunity of a final rousing cymbal clash. It was to be Harold's big moment.

As the bandmaster accelerated the closing bars, he glanced to see if Harold was ready. Harold was too ready. Bringing up his right hand, he hit the cymbal prematurely on the upswing. He desperately reached over with his left hand to quieten the mistake, but as he did so, his knee knocked the bass drum off its stand. Down it rolled and bumped off the platform into the laps of the surprised front pew occupants.

To my knowledge, the band was never asked again to play in that church.

We did, however, travel to the town of Powell River where the C.O. had arranged a march of witness. It would take us through the picturesque town, built on a mountain slope, down towards the sea. On such a march, Harold, our somewhat timid drummer at the rear of the march, had to be encouraged not so much to pat but to beat the drum.

Marching up a particularly steep hill we noticed the drum sounding fainter. "Hit it harder, Harold," we yelled. As we neared the top and rounded the corner of the adjoining street, we saw the reason for the diminuendo. There at the bottom of the hill sat Harold, too tired to march further, but still valiantly trying to thwack his drum.

He did what all good drummers do: he became Flag Sergeant. Remembrance Day came. The Army band always took part in the march and cenotaph service. Our newly-commissioned flag man took his place at the head of the band, beaming proudly. As the band played the tune of "Onward, Christian Soldiers," Harold stepped out boldly as though all Christendom rested on his shoulders.

But I suddenly noticed that the band seemed to be stopping playing. Section by section they shut down, first the trombones, then some of the horns and cornets. The cause: our flag bearer.

Harold had put on weight since first getting his uniform. The exertion of carrying the flag, plus the extra pounds, had burst whatever it was that had been holding up his trousers. Taking to heart his responsibility to "lift up the banner on high" and "never let the old flag fall," Harold was hobbling down the street in a vain attempt to hold both the flag and his pants, by now around his ankles.

A Remembrance Day to remember indeed!

CHAPTER 13

ALL ONE BODY WE

RELATIONSHIPS BETWEEN THE SALVATION ARMY and the other churches have not always been as cordial as they appear to be now.

William Booth, the Army's Founder, felt that in the main the churches had never shown him the slightest encouragement. Even when as a teenager, full of evangelical zeal, he marched into the Wesley Chapel with what historian Robert Sandall describes as "a tatterdemalion contingent from the Nottingham slums" behind him, he was criticized. The deacons peremptorily told him that if he brought such a flock into the chapel again, they must sit behind a partition which shielded them off from the pulpit, and on benches without backs or cushions.

Because he wanted to devote much of his time to open-air work on the streets and greens, he asked for his name to be removed from the list of local preachers but to continue as a church member. The Methodist Church was undergoing acrimonious controversy at the time and the minister of Booth's circuit concluded that William was a rebel. So he

167

curtly withheld his ticket of membership. Booth later commented that the agitation in the main concerned ecclesiastical questions for which he did not care a penny.

Later (in 1882) the Church of England was to pay a remarkable tribute to Booth's Army when it suggested discussions about the possibility of the Army coming under the wing of the Anglican Church. Bishop Lightfoot wrote about the Army: "Whatever may be its faults, it had at least recalled us to the lost ideal of the Church, the universal compulsion of the souls of men." The discussions went ahead at a high level, but gradually petered out. Booth, his son Bramwell, and that first Commissioner, George Scott Railton, feared that that same ecclesiolatry would stifle the Army's essential mobility and singleness of purpose.

~

A NUN TO THE RESCUE

Major David E. Cedervall advises that along the Mississippi River there are often calls for Salvation Army disaster service as the "Muddy Miss" overflows her banks and floods river towns. One of these is Dubuque, Iowa, a community which has a high percentage of Roman Catholic churches, schools and other institutions.

During a flood in the 1960s, a group of nuns volunteered to serve in the Army mobile canteen on its feeding runs to National Guard troops and other emergency personnel. Usually, the markings on the canteen and other Army identification opened doors into closed areas, but this time a young National Guard sentry stopped the Army officer driver. He was not going to allow the canteen to continue beyond his checkpoint.

One of the nuns in the back of the canteen looked up from the food trays she was sorting and recognized the guard as a former student from her teaching days in the Catholic school.

She opened the sliding door window, eased her head out with her habit in clear view and demanded, "Listen John! You

let us through right now. We are from The Salvation Army."
HE DID!

PERSISTENT PRESBYTERIAN

Now back in his USA homeland and retired,
Commissioner David A. Baxendale sportlingly assures me I
may recount what happened to him when, as Colonel, he
addressed a large congregation in a Presbyterian church. After
giving his sermon, he went with the pastor to greet members
of the congregation at the main door.

Knowing that most churches have their own "Silly Billy,"
the good Colonel was not too startled when one little old
man, shaking his hand, said, "You spoke too long!" But then
he ran around, got in line and came through a second time.
Again another vigorous handshake and this time he commented, "You spoke too loud!"

The pastor seemed to take no notice as the little man ran
back yet again to get in line and shake the Salvation Army
guest's hand. This third time his choice word was, "Besides
that, you didn't say anything!"

By this time, the pastor was taking notice. "Colonel, don't
pay any attention to him. He just repeats what everybody else
is saying!"

THE R.C. HOSPITAL CHART

The irrepressible Colonel Rowland D. Hughes tells of a
Salvation Army officer who, while visiting a Roman Catholic
hospital, glanced idly at a wall chart in the ward sister's office
while waiting for her to return from attending to a patient.

"I see you have mostly Roman Catholics in your ward, sister," he remarked when she returned.

"Why do you say that?" she asked, looking puzzled.

"Because on your wall chart I see that after nearly all the
names are the initials 'RC.' Only one name has a 'P' after it."

She laughed merrily. "That's the breakfast list for tomorrow morning. Seventeen patients want Rice Crispies and only one wants porridge."

COMMISSIONER WESLEY HARRIS, now enjoying retirement in Australia, recalls two ecumenical occasions:

"YOU'RE ON MY SASH"

As area commander in Exeter, England, I shared in a significant gathering at Exeter Cathedral, where the principal guest was HM Queen Elizabeth the Queen Mother. The Army's public relations officer, Major Joseph Wright, and I joined the procession of bishops and other religious leaders before the two of us were placed in seats quite near the royal party. Sharing the pew with us was the monsignor of the Roman Catholic church.

We knelt together during the time of prayer, then stood for the hymn which immediately followed—that is, except for the monsignor, who remained kneeling, apparently bent in further prayer.

I was momentarily impressed by the good man's deep devotion, then I saw him look up with anxious face to Joe Wright: "Excuse me," he whispered, "you're standing on my sash."

ECUMENICAL ANAGRAMS

I remember a time in Dunblane, Scotland, when the Archbishop of Canterbury was the special preacher. A group of church leaders was seated before a congregation of perhaps a thousand people, waiting for the service to begin.

On my right was the Rev. Dr. Lord McCleod, whose name will always be associated with the Iona community. At over eighty years of age, he remained something of a rebel and also a humorist.

Surveying the scene, he muttered out of the corner of his mouth, "Do you know the anagram for 'episcopal'?" I shook my head slightly.

With the caption, "Pulling a Pint," this cartoon was used on a Christmas card in Britain. Neither the bull pictured on the pub's signboard nor the drinking patrons seem to be showing much good cheer. Cartoon by courtesy of artist Dick Millington and Royle Publications Limited.

Cartoonist Franklin sees British political figures—Prime Minister/Foreign Secretary Douglas Hume, Chancellor Reginald Maudlin and Quintin Hogg—as fervent Salvationists promising heaven on earth if the electorate will vote Tory (Conservative). Courtesy of *The Sun* newspaper.

When the Army's famous "Joy Strings" pop group took the gospel message into London's notorious "Blue Angel" night club, cartoonist Franklin envisioned angelic transformations in the patrons. Courtesy of *The Sun* newspaper.

Past No. 10 Downing Street, home of the Prime Minister, marches a Salvation Army, including Quintin Hogg, Harold Macmillan, Edward Heath, Harold Wilson and Margaret Thatcher. (The latter four all became Prime Minister). Inside No. 10, guarded by a policeman, Prime Minister James Callaghan wrestles with Britain's "winter of discontent." The London Bobby sends in the message to him: "Tell Jim The Salvation Army is here!" Each of the marchers was wanting his job. Cartoon by Franklin, courtesy of *The Sun* newspaper.

"Tell Jim The Salvation Army is here!"

A cartoon that appeared in both France and Germany. Titled, "Theatre of War," it speaks of a king calling his vassals to go to war—i.e. The Salvation Army under General Booth is giving a war cry.

From Davidson Brothers pictorial postcards "Illustrated Songs" series, printed in Bavaria.

General Booth—"A few Salvation services here wouldn't hurt, I think!"

Less than 20 years after beginning his East End of London ministry, William Booth was hitting the headlines. His national protest about the abduction of young girls into prostitution and his fearless questioning of morality in the highest echelons of society evoked these two cartoons (and several more) from "The Entr'acte"—an illustrated theatrical and musical review which under several titles was published in London between 1869 and 1907.

John Bull— "Now, then, Mr. Booth, tell us the truth about this abduction case!"

Britain's "winter of discontent" in the '60s provoked some violent solutions by political parties with extremist views. Cartoonist CHRYS joked that the situation was so dire the only answer might be the intervention of The Salvation Army. Courtesy of the *News of the World*.

"It's Pepsi Cola," he replied. Then, "Do you know the one for 'Presbyterian'?"

Again, I shook my head and endeavored to keep a straight face.

"It's best in prayer," he whispered.

I was just waiting for the great and endearingly mischievous man to come up with an anagram for "The Salvation Army" when, perhaps mercifully, the service began.

CHAPTER 14

ALL PART OF THE JOB

B RAMWELL BOOTH, SON OF THE ARMY'S FOUNDER, his Chief of Staff and successor, wrote a 165-page book in 1899 designed "to set forth something of the inner life and character of officers of The Salvation Army." He believed that an understanding of the Movement's officers would give the general public a better understanding of the Movement.

The thought may also have crossed his mind that in describing the dedication, the passionate evangelism, the long hours, the poverty, and the unstinting practical concern of his officers, he would also be writing a statement of what he expected Army officers to be.

He called the book *Servants of All*. There was no doubt in his mind that if an officer wanted to be a servant of God, he or she would have to accept the burden and challenge of being the servant of all. Since the Lord and Savior the officer professed to follow had declared He had come to minister, not to be ministered unto, then the disciple had better follow suit.

But just how far must you be willing to become "servant of all"?

The question was not in the mind of Major Graham Grayston, of Pokesdown, Bournemouth, when the telephone rang insistently at his bedside at 4 a.m. Groping desperately to organize his thinking, Graham heard a man's voice asking if that was The Salvation Army. Graham's mind was sufficiently clear to answer "Yes."

"Good! Is my wife there?" asked the voice.

"What makes you think she might be?" queried Graham, with no thought of checking that the slumbering form beside him was that of his wife, Margaret.

"Well, you're The Salvation Army, aren't you?"

"We are indeed," agreed Graham, "but we're not a hostel. This is a private house."

"Well, I'm worried about my wife. She's gone missing."

"How long has she been missing?"

"Two years."

"Two years! Couldn't your call have waited until tomorrow morning? In any case, you need to telephone our Missing Persons' Department."

"O.K. Give me the number."

"The telephone number is on my file downstairs in the office. It may interest you to know that I'm in bed. In any case, the Missing Persons Department is in London and doesn't open until eight-thirty in the morning."

"Ah, well. Never mind. I'll get the number from the telephone directory."

Since telephones were not installed in officers' quarters in 1899, Bramwell Booth's book did not include a chapter on 4 a.m. callers. Major Grayston might well have wished for such guidance when just a few nights later, at 2 a.m., a drunk phoned to offer a quantity of old clothes for the charity shop.

Graham seems to attract very late night or early morning calls, for there was also a misdirected call to his home at 5 a.m. from Dunfermline, Scotland, apologizing that "Mary won't be able to come in today." Graham discovered that but for one digit he had the identical number of a Scottish post office.

When Graham answered a daytime call it was from a distressed lady asking if he could provide her a food parcel. Her weekly Post Office Giro cheque had not arrived.

"What part of Bournemouth do you live in?" he asked.

"Bournemouth? Who said anything about Bournemouth? I live in Potters Bar. I must have got the wrong number."

Graham is of the opinion that his early-day predecessors without telephones may well have found it easier in some ways to be servants of all.

~~

BRAMWELL BOOTH'S SERVANTS OF ALL *was a little masterpiece that made a powerful impact in his day. Only six months later, a second printing was needed, such had been the demand. Readers declared it to be a moving story of "common lives beautified, exalted, ennobled by a lofty purpose."*

The stories that follow, like those concerning the Graystons, obviously don't merit that kind of eulogy. But they do give an insight into the everyday affairs of the present-day Salvation Army officer and soldier, and a glimpse of how Mr. and Mrs. Public regard the Army. And Mr. and Mrs. Salvation Army must continue on their unflappable way, regarding such happenings as "ALL PART OF THE JOB."

~~

OUR MAN AT GATWICK

With typical ingenuity, Commissioner Denis Hunter sought a position as chaplain at London's busy Gatwick Airport when he retired from the demanding positions of British Commissioner and then International Secretary for Africa. Here, he would not only take turns with other chaplains in conducting regular advertised services for travelers in the airport chapel but, still more importantly in his view, be available to give counsel and guidance to any who sought his help as he strolled amidst the bustling crowds wearing his full Army uniform. He called such strolls his "availability walkabout."

"Do you think I might be able to buy a black tie here at the airport?" one traveler asked him. "Perhaps in the Burton's store, just there," Denis responded. Then wondering about the cause of the request and wanting to be helpful he asked, "Are you traveling on a sad journey then, sir?"

The man grinned. "No, not at all. My son-in-law supports Stoke City Football Club and they've just been demoted to a lower division. I wanted to send him an appropriate symbol."

He was moving through the International Departure Lounge when a lady hailed him. "Isn't it possible now to buy nuts at Gatwick? I promised my friend here that they have delicious nuts at the airport."

Commissioner Hunter explained that the nut stand was landside. The two ladies were now airside. But, servant of all that he was, would they like him to return landside for them to negotiate the purchase of such highly desirable edibles? (Denis has quite a flow of language!)

"Would you really!" they enthused. "Then a quarter of cashew nuts, if you please. Here is £2."

The mission was duly accomplished, a receipt for £1.98 secured, and our chaplain reported back to the departure lounge. The delight of the travelers knew no bounds as Denis handed over the bounty, together with the 2 pence, half expecting them to say, "Oh no, put that in the box." But not so. Budgeting was obviously the name of the game.

"I subscribe regularly to your great organization," said the lady, as she put the 2p coin in her purse. Then with this financial transaction completed, she and her friend settled down to enjoy some mouth-watering munching moments.

~

THE HEAVENLY HOME

The divisions and disagreements among the "comrades" in his corps caused a Commanding Officer much heartache and worry. One Sunday night he issued a challenge to his congregation: "All those who want to go to heaven, raise your right hand." Every right hand in the citadel was lifted high.

But the C.O. remained at attention, his own hands at his side. The Corps Sergeant Major leapt to his feet to question him: "Don't you want to go to heaven, Major?"

In decisive tones the Major replied: "Yes, I certainly do, Sergeant Major, but not with this lot."

—*John Thompson, Brigadier (R)*

SNIPPETS

As young officers, we had just been transferred to Wichita, Kansas, when the following advertisement appeared in the classified section of the *Wichita Beacon* newspaper:

"Anyone interested in joining a nudist colony, please contact us by calling (phone number)…"

Directly below, the following advertisement read:

"Give your cast-off clothing to The Salvation Army. Just call (phone number)"

—*Dorothy Justvig, Lt.-Colonel (R)*

The corps officer was praying in a meeting when she became aware that a member of the congregation had fainted. "Just a minute, Lord, May's gone," she intoned, and ran to May's assistance.

—*Theo Kitching, Lt.-Colonel (from Joy Kitching)*

When Major Woodrow Wilson Pryor arrived to take charge of the corps in Johnson City, Tennessee, one of the first Salvationists to greet him was my father, Corps Sergeant Major Theodore Roosevelt Arrowood.

Throughout Major Pryor's stay at Johnson City, the congregation liked to assert that both Republican and Democrat parties were well represented.

—*Henry Arrowood, Major*

During a recent holiness meeting, our corps officer was preaching fervently on the subject of the unleavened bread.

Abruptly, he paused and flung out the rhetorical question, "Now, what is leaven?"

Before I could stop myself and without thinking (as usual!), I called out: "Halfway between ten and twelve."

—*Ben Meyer, Major (R)*

Three snippets from the memory of *Lt.-Colonel Houston Ellis (R)*:

Some years ago, an officer in West Virginia was asked to conduct a wedding ceremony for a man and woman who had come in from the hills with several of their children. When the officer asked why such a long delay in making the union legal, the man replied, "The roads were so bad."

An officer received a scribbled postcard from a woman. It read: "If you handle the adoption of children, will you put a small girl on the 3:10 p.m. bus next Wednesday. I will meet it when it gets to town and adopt her!"

An occasional attendee at a corps wanted to complain to his Divisional Commander about the corps officer. She was pouring out her problem over the telephone, telling on which Sunday the alleged incident had taken place.

"You know," she explained, "it was the Sunday when they bumped the flags together." (In the States, new soldiers are sworn in under both American and Salvation Army flags.)

Two snippets from *Sweeping Through the Land*:

In Cumberland, MD, on her regular *War Cry* rounds, the Captain was told by a customer, "My goat loves to eat *The War Cry* but won't touch our newspaper, *The Independent*."

The officer handed the customer a copy of *The War Cry*, which the goat promptly ate.

Next week the customer told her: "That *War Cry* put new life into my goat. He just caught me between his horns and threw me against the gate. Now he works spendidly!"

Captain McAfee, of Anniston, Alabama, reported on an open-air meeting attended by a large crowd. When two of the Salvationists were called on to sing a duet, a buggy pulled up to listen. As the singers reached the chorus, the mule joined in and continued to bray each time the women reached the chorus. He quit when the song was over.

~~

WHATSOEVER STATE

We were traveling by Pullman train in Japan, assigned to a compartment with two sets of three-tier bunks on either side. Our translator scrambled up to the top bunk; my husband occupied the middle bunk; and I was happy to have the lowest level. Only a curtain hung across each bunk. The voices, groans, snores were heard by all but, in true Japanese style, ignored.

I climbed into my space. It seemed to be about eighteen inches wide and less than six feet long. It was a challenge to find a place for my suitcase, handbag, coat, bonnet, and stand-up collar uniform. I soon realized as I shifted and turned that it would be the better part of wisdom to remove only my outer garment and just be thankful for a place to stretch out for the long bumpy journey. It was not possible to sit up straight, the accommodation having been evidently made for smaller people.

After some time I wiggled into a prone position with my feet resting on my suitcase. I reached for my Bible wanting to know if there was "a word from the Lord" for me. What I read set me off into peals of laughter. My husband and the translator wanted to know what was funny. I read to them from Philippians 4:11:

"I have learned in whatsoever state I am, therewith to be content."

Once again, I was convinced that the Lord has a marvelous sense of humor.

—*Katherine Rightmire, Mrs. Commissioner (R)*

≈

BATHING COSTUME INVADERS

When the first party of Salvation Army officers left England for Japan in 1895, I had been responsible for the provision of Japanese uniforms to be worn on arrival. I sought the advice of Mr. Fry, a well-known Quaker missionary, who had been in Japan for years, and we copied the one he thought best from his own uniform.

On their way to Japan, these pioneer officers called at Hong Kong where, doubtful whether the dress provided was just the right thing, they hastily had kimonos made for each member of the party. The tailor, in good faith, provided them with the kind used in Japan only for bathing. Those pioneers caused very great amusement when they landed in the equivalent of bathing costumes.

—*from* A Missionary's Memories, *by Commissioner Henry Bullard*

≈

THE FIGHT ON SECOND STREET

My first corps appointment after serving on the training school staff was Eureka, California. Populated by loggers, millworkers and commercial fishermen, it was also during World War II a naval air base, dry docks and a Coast Guard station—in other words, a town where "men were men."

On a Sunday evening, the faithful and I were conducting our regular open-air meeting on Second Street, where every other door opened to a bar and each second floor housed prostitutes.

Part way through our service, a fellow stopped in front of the ring of Salvationists and spewed out a mouthful of foul language. I could see that although he was not drunk, he had been drinking, so I asked him to move on and not disturb the meeting.

In a few minutes he was back with more vile language

than before. Our group included a lovely retired school teacher, a young secretary and other sensitive people who should never be subject to such filth. Again—a bit stronger this time—I urged him to move on and leave us alone.

At once he came toward me threateningly with an angry expression. The dilemma: to take a beating or give one. In a split second's decision, I opted for the latter. I handed my glasses and Bible to someone in the ring and met him halfway. Fortunately, I landed the first punch and sent him flying against the wall of the bar. I pulled him up on his feet and again commanded him not to talk like that in front of my people.

As I turned to go back to the open-air ring, he took a swing at me. I sensed it coming and ducked. My turn. I hit him again and he landed in a heap in the doorway of the bar. The police came and took him. I tried to talk them out of charging him but they would have none of it. "The Army has been here for over fifty years and we won't stand for anyone giving them trouble."

Meantime "Fight!" had echoed along Second Street. All the inhabitants came to see. The Coast Guard cutter had just brought in a load of servicemen from the base. Traffic was halted and the sidewalk was a sea of men. After the police and our heckler were gone, I continued to lead our street meeting, taking advantage of such an audience.

On the way back to the hall, everyone was quiet. My mind was in turmoil: surely headquarters would hear about my fight and I would be farewelled, perhaps without appointment. After a while, old Brother Bill—a retired logger with a bushy beard of gray hair and a strong face—started mumbling. "Never seen anything like it. Never seen anything like it."

My fears increased. Then he stopped, placed a big hand squarely on my shoulder and said again, "Never seen anything like it, Cap. If we could get a crowd like that, you ought to have a fight every Sunday night."

At our open-air meeting the following Wednesday

evening, I asked our regular Second Street congregation why *they* hadn't ushered our heckler away. Their answer: "Cap., he was looking for trouble. If we'd got into a fight with him, we'd have been thrown into jail. But we knew they wouldn't throw you in jail."

—*Gene Rice, Lt.-Colonel (R)*

〜

"I'D LIKE TO TAKE HIM FOR A RIDE"

As a very young Captain, I was in charge of a corps in a headquarters city. There was urgent need of a car: it was harvest festival time and the Lieutenant and I needed a conveyance to collect produce from farmers for our harvest festival sale.

I went to the used car dealer who had provided autos for other Salvation Army officers. He had no Ford Model A on the lot—which was what I could afford—but he had a ten-year-old De Soto which he would sell me for the same price, $125. So, mission accomplished, except for the fact that I had not secured permission from the Divisional Commander, a requirement of regulation even though an officer had to pay for a car personally in those good old days!

The D.C. had been out of the town at the time of the transaction. As soon as he returned, I went to see him, hoping for the belated sanction. His first word was to remind me of the approved makes of car that officers could purchase. De Soto was not on the list. I pled my case, arguing that the De Soto was a much better car than a Model A, particularly because it had hydraulic brakes, not the mechanical brakes of the Ford. The Colonel was adamant. The Commissioner would never give approval.

In a final petition I wailed, "Colonel, I'd like to take the Commissioner for a ride in my De Soto and show him what a fine car it is."

In his clipped way the Colonel responded, *"Sister, a lot of people would like to take the Commissioner for a ride."* End of interview!

Sequel: I took my fine De Soto back to the dealer who by then had a Model A Ford, which he kindly traded evenly for the De Soto.

—*Hazel Rice, Mrs. Lt.-Colonel (R)*

WELL WORTH A DIME

A uniformed Salvationist couple, having attended a meeting held in a large hotel, were riding to the lobby in the elevator. Also in the lift were other guests of the hotel attending a convention. Some of them had evidently been imbibing enough to be slightly inebriated.

As the car stopped at the lobby and the Salvationist couple stepped out, one of the group began to sing loudly, raucously, a song that has been used derisively against Salvationists:

"Put a nickel on the drum;
Save another drunken bum;
Oh, Hallelujah"

With that the woman Salvationist turned to them and said sweetly:

"So you're the one
those nickels are from;
Most people give at least a dime,
Why don't you, the very next time?"

—*Ernest A. Miller, Colonel (R)*

LIGHTS OUT

John Will Pattison and Tom Plumber were early-day converts in the ancient city of Durham, each of whom ultimately became the mayor. Soon after conversion, they were made envoys and frequently traveled to appointments together.

One late autumn Sunday they went to a Sunderland corps. After an encouraging but busy day, they set off for home on their bicycles. It was a dark, rain-dampening evening. Just before they reached Houghton-le-Spring, one had a puncture. They walked on down the dark hill to the first street lamp and began the repair. Several people passed by without showing interest, not even offering an encouraging word. This was hardly just reward for a full day toiling for the Lord.

But then things improved. An old man walking with the aid of a stick stopped to inquire what was the trouble. He chatted for some minutes, then exclaimed, "Well, lads, I am sorry, but I can't stay here all night." With that, with his stick he put the gas light out.

He was the lamp-lighter.

—*Leslie Piper*

UNDER COVER OPERATION: Lt.-Colonel John Dale's experiment:

When the doctor advised me to undergo an operation and a period of recuperation in the hospital, I sensed that here was a good chance to make an experiment. I could use the opportunity to contribute something to the debate as to whether or not our uniform creates a barrier to reaching people for Christ.

So, taking my non-Blood-and-Fire pajamas, I arrived at the hospital in civvies and was soon in bed, with not a sign of religion anywhere. This, I thought, would help me to get nearer to the other patients. I would be more acceptable. Just one of them.

The first salvo from my fellow patients came that evening: would I make up a foursome in a game of cards? Having never played cards, I politely declined. There was a slight cooling of what had previously been a warm atmosphere. Putting on my dressing-gown, I tried a little friendly conversation.

The next invitation was to have a smoke. "We have a secret rendezvous," was the confidential aside as they made their exit. Again I apologized.

Later we were tucked up in bed for the night when there came the final salvo of the day—an invitation to have a beer! Harry, in the corner bed, was a long-time patient and the drinks organizer. ("It looks good, it tastes good, and by golly it does yer good!") A wink and a cheery nod accompanied the offer. Again, I had to refuse, and a sickly feeling added to my discomfort. The arrival of a precocious night-worker who was well acquainted with my friends made me realize I was not part of their conversational world.

That night I did not sleep too well. I wondered if I had been right to come in incognito. But the next morning settled the issue. It was an important day in the horse-racing world, Derby Day. The whole ward was highly animated.

"Have a flutter," they suggested persuasively. "We all do it." I was treated to the points count on all the horses and encouraged to put my bet on one which was a "dead cert."

I let the excitement of the day settle down and then made my confession. I told them that I was the local Salvation Army Captain and, although I could not join in many of their activities, I nevertheless wanted to be friends with them.

"Why didn't you tell us in the first place?" was the unanimous chorus.

In the convalescing days ahead there were little strolls, good natured exchanges of views, friendly arguments and one-to-one conversations about the Christian faith. I was encouraged and strengthened and given a renewed zest for life. I was in the right place, at the right time, with the right people.

I had been home only a week when, early one Sunday morning, the telephone rang. It was the hospital matron. "Harry wants to see you. It's urgent."

Arriving at the hospital I was hurriedly ushered into a small single ward. "Glad you've come," was Harry's greeting. He looked very ill. His fight against cancer was coming to an end. I read the Shepherd's Psalm and quoted the comforting words from John 14: "In my Father's house are many mansions…I go to prepare a place for you…that where I am, there you may be also."

"Do you believe that promise is for you, Harry?" I asked him very softly and tenderly. He nodded his assent.

We joined in prayer and I committed Harry to the love and mercy of God. Then I opened my eyes. But his eyes had finally closed. He was just going into the presence of his newly-found Savior and Lord. I was glad to be in uniform.

~

IN HIS RETIREMENT YEARS, Lt.-Colonel John Dale accepted service as a prison chaplain. Here are three of his recollections:

When visiting the prison workshop I noticed that Bill, usually a very cheerful-looking fellow, was looking decidedly glum. "What's the problem, Bill?" I inquired. "You look sad."

"I've every right to be sad," replied Bill. "Would you believe it, while I'm in here doing my time, someone has burgled my apartment."

"What are you in here for, Bill?" I asked.

"Burglary," was the unashamed reply.

The Christmas pantomime, presented for the prisoners and by the prisoners, was always a keenly anticipated event. It would be performed some five times to audiences that included invited guests, schools and "oldies" clubs. Probably the most successful pantomime was the one with a very popular title: "Ali Baba and the Forty Thieves." There was no shortage of applicants for the cast.

Sam—a fine, well-built giant of a man with a perpetual smile and a bigger-than-life personality—had recently become a born-again Christian. As usual, he greeted me with a powerful handshake. I tried to hide my discomfort, accepting the heartiness of the greeting.

"You know, John," he said to me with great enthusiasm, "the Lord brought me here." My immediate reaction was to point out that I didn't think the Lord was in the business of embarrassing the government by overcrowding the prisons. Instead I congratulated him on his new-found faith and added, "I think, Sam, it was your misdeeds that brought you here, but the Lord has been able to use even your folly to give new meaning to your life."

"Right on, John," Sam replied, "right on." And he went singing on his way.

"DO YOU STILL SING?"

Friday night might mean "TGIF Night" (Thank God it's Friday) for many people, but for Salvation Army Captain Bramwell Pratt, Commanding Officer of Morriston Corps in South Wales, it meant the seven-mile bus ride to the village of Ystraglynlais, there to sell *The War Cry* and other Army periodicals in the public houses.

The bus was always packed to capacity. As Bram stood holding his bundle of papers with one hand, and clinging tight with his other to keep his balance in the swaying bus, a lady crushed against him asked if she could buy a *War Cry*. He managed to execute the sale without dropping the bundle or falling onto the lap of the seated passenger by him.

"Do you still sing when you sell the papers?" asked the lady.

"Yes, indeed we do," answered the Army man.

"Do you sing 'Power in the Blood'?"

"Er, yes. That and many others."

"Oh, good. That's my favorite. Would you sing it now?"

"What, now?" repeated Bram, aghast at the idea. "The bus company probably wouldn't allow me to do that kind of thing," he replied, seizing on any excuse.

"If you started it up, everybody would join in," she assured him in her lilting Welsh accent.

Bram could see there was no escape. He cleared his throat and began:

Would you be free from your burden of sin?
There's power in the Blood, power in the Blood....

No conductor of a Welsh choir ever had more responsive vocalists. Far above the roaring of the bus engine every delighted passenger joined in with full-throated, four-part harmony:

Would you o'er evil a victory win?
There's wonderful pow'r in the Blood.

Well, it was Wales, after all, and these English Captains needed to be taught a thing or two!

~~

HOW DO YOU DO IT, GENERAL?

The newly elected General Eva Burrows was on an introductory whistle-stop tour across Canada. A group of vivacious young timbrelists from Santa Ana, in Southern California, had flown to Vancouver, British Columbia, for her welcome meetings there. Every event attracted a capacity attendance. The excitement at the Army only now having a woman General again after forty seven years since the retirement of General Evangeline Booth was intense.

General Burrows preached with passion and power in the Sunday morning meeting. As she was leaving the rented theater, the group of American teenage timbrelists blocked her way. "Oh, General," they cried excitedly, "we want to ask you a question."

No doubt they want clarification of a theological point in the General's sermon, thought the territorial leaders with her. "Fire away," she invited with a smile.

"General, we hope you won't mind us asking, but how do you do your hair?" they asked, patting her hair approvingly. And the General who moments before had been preaching powerfully and passionately, now revealed the secrets of her haute coiffure.

CHAPTER 15

'TWAS THE MONTH BEFORE CHRISTMAS

I WAS ELEVEN YEARS OLD when my officer parents were appointed in charge of The Salvation Army's ministry at the heart of grimy old Manchester, in the industrial north of England. They called the area where we lived, "All Saints." No wonder! You had to be one to live there.

My mother, born and bred amidst the lush green countryside of Cornwall in southwest England, fought a losing battle with the soot that showered down upon her white lace curtains from the common lodging houses opposite our quarters. Street cars—steel-throated monsters running on rails sunk into the roadway—rattled and bashed their way past our front doorstep from dawn till well after midnight.

Our three story house, with dank, awesome, cavernous cellar below, was tightly sandwiched between one of England's dark satanic mills on one side and the Salvation Army hall on the other. Our left hand wall reverberated with the ceaseless thump of clattering looms. Our right hand wall syncopated with the oompah, oompah of senior and young people's bands rehearsing their gospel melodies designed to save the world.

As an eleven-year-old boy, I quickly discovered the advantages of living right next door to the Salvation Army hall. One moment I could be late lying abed, resisting my mother's increasingly agitated calls to get up. In next to no time, I could be fully clothed if not in my right mind, attending morning Sunday school.

My poor father quickly discovered the disadvantages of living next door to his place of worship. Whenever anything was needed by his industrious but often forgetful Salvationists, they would immediately ring our front doorbell.

Tea, milk, sugar, soap, a spare tambourine? "Go and ask the Major." Fuses, matches, candles when the electricity failed? "Go and ask the Major." With seemingly infinite patience, my father made no protest. Were not Salvation Army majors ordained by God to provide sugar, soap, matches, fuse-wire?

He preferred those requests to the more demanding occasions when some ruffian in that down-at-heel area would walk into the halls and threaten trouble. Then, very urgently, the Salvationists would say, "Fetch the Major."

Or even those times when his zealous workers would let their quick tempers and strong passions forget the availability of divine grace and there would be fierce discord among them. Then still more urgently would one of them say, "We'd better fetch the Major." At such times my father's tact and never-failing sense of humor did not let him down.

One year, close to Christmas, when feeling utterly exhausted through extra heavy work and preparation for the essential Christmas caring program, father resolved to go to bed early. "And they'd better not disturb me tonight," he growled ominously as he made his way up the stairs to his bedroom at the unusually early hour of 9 p.m.

"They" were the bandsmen and other workers who were painting the scenery and putting up the stage drapes for the nativity play organized every year by Jim Redhead. Folk traveled from miles around to see Jim Redhead's productions. Jim was a fine fellow. You could trust Jim to handle everything. Father felt that his good night's sleep was assured.

Alas, his head had scarcely touched the pillow when the doorbell rang. Mother answered, then apprehensively climbed the stairs to tell father he was needed. With a weariness beyond description he put on his old red dressing gown and wonderingly went down the stairs.

Young Willy Pritchard stood at the door. Seventeen-year-old Willy did not need extra-sensory perception to detect that he was not really welcome.

"Well, what is it?" growled father in a tone that would have done credit to Scrooge. "What is it this time?"

"P-p-please, Major," said Willy, stammering in his nervousness, "Jim Redhead said would I fetch the Major."

Sudden totally unaccustomed anger filled my father. He sped upstairs like an Olympic sprinter, pulled navy serge trousers over protesting pajamas, grabbed his tunic and, not stopping to comb his tousled hair, rushed out of the house slamming the door behind him. "I'll tell them this time," he muttered to himself as he went, "I'll tell them this time."

Still at breakneck speed he rushed into the hall and, like an Old Testament prophet, demanded, "What is it this time? What on earth do you want me for at this time of night?"

The good Jim Redhead stopped sawing a plank of wood and a look of astonishment spread over his honest face. "I-I-I don't understand," he began, but his voice petered out into aba-aba sounds.

Father swung round with accusing finger to where Willy Pritchard cowered. That young man found his voice. "But-but-but you told me, Mr. Redhead, you told me to fetch the Major."

There was a moment of silence that seemed like eternity. Slowly Jim Redhead buckled at the knees and sank to the floor, gurgling both with laughter and groans.

Finally, while everyone else looked on in amazement, Jim—his shoulders heaving with mirth—spluttered, "Oh,

Major, dear Major, I didn't tell Willy to fetch the Major, I told him to 'FETCH THE MANGER'."

~

CALIFORNIA, birthplace of so many original ideas, is credited with being the first USA state to have on its streets the now famous and ubiquitous Christmas kettle to raise funds for the Army's winter relief program for the needy. The first kettle appeared on the Oakland Ferry Wharf in 1891, with the aim of financing "Christmas Dinner for 1000." There's little doubt that the kettles were well-used following the 1906 San Francisco earthquake, which devastated the West Coast city and produced a monumental response of compassionate and innovative aid for the stricken from, what was until then, a little-known movement still in its infancy.

An enterprising officer saw in the idea of a simple kettle on a stand a natural unspoken appeal to the public to "Keep the pot boiling" during the season of good will. A special advantage is that the kettle need not be manned by a Salvationist. Any warm-hearted friend can take a turn for a couple of hours in standing by the kettle and ringing the little Christmas silver bell that summons the public to generosity. Members of Rotary, Kiwanis and other public-spirited clubs will vie with each other in raising the largest sums for the Army's ministry. For many in the States, Christmas has not really begun until those bells begin to tinkle.

During his term of responsibility for The Salvation Army in Salinas, California, Captain Moses Reyes evoked great regard from the local citizens for the quality and devotion of his service to people in all kinds of need. The local Chamber of Commerce gave him its "Man of the Year" award. His own advisory board proudly supported him with a score of major schemes. And when Christmas time came, there was no hesitation from even the most distinguished members in taking turn in manning the humble kettles on the streets.

Even the chairman, though a member of the Jewish faith,

cheerfully rang the Christmas bell and stood beside the Christmas kettle.

A member of his own synagogue passing by found the incongruity of the situation somewhat amusing. From across the street he called to his friend, "Hey, what are you doing ringing that bell for Christmas?"

"I'm not ringing this bell for Christmas," the chairman shouted back. "I'M RINGING IT FOR MOSES."

SUCCESS IN BELL-RINGING IN NORTH AMERICA, street collecting with a box in Europe while Army bandsmen play carols, or selling tags for the annual appeal anywhere in the world depends most of all on the quality of the collector: personality, appearance, tactful boldness, cheerfulness and wit determine the amount in the kettle and the box. Such qualities, or their absence, also determine whether for the collector the experience is just a dutiful miserable chore or rollicking good fun.

Major David E. Cedervall, of the USA Eastern Territory, recalls the reaction of a Commanding Officer when he learned that a shopping mall management would give permission for the location of Christmas kettles only if they were manned by kettle attendants. "In order to eliminate intrusive noise possibilities, not even the smallest bells shall be rung."

The Commanding Officer, Captain Keith Dawnley, expressed disappointment but finally agreed to make the best of the situation. So, he took a bell, removed the clapper, stood by the kettle and went through the ringing motions. No sound was emitted by the shiny tool so famed in Christmas legend and song.

Shoppers begin to walk by. They notice the familiar sight out of the corner of their eyes but don't realize the familiar tinkling sound is missing.

Then a young man does a double take, walks closer getting change out of his pocket and asks, "Why is your bell not making any sound?"

"It's playing 'Silent Night'," replies the Captain.

The shopper chuckles, drops the money in the kettle and moves on down the mall.

Captain Dawnley watches a couple approaching. He sees the wife is realizing the bell is silent. He grins as they pass by. He notices the lady say something to the man. They both turn, see the Captain smiling at them, grin back and continue on their way. Later they return and put money in the kettle. The wife asks, "Why no jingle in your bell?"

"I guess it's a DUMB bell!" The Captain smiles and they laugh together.

A business man comes along, realizes that the lack of sound and picture are not consistent, and takes a longer look. He fumbles for a dollar note and as he drops it into the kettle he points at the bell.

"Is it broken?"

"No, it's on strike for higher wages, but it's still doing well!"

A mother with three youngsters goes by, the kids each taking a peek at the money in the kettle. Mom stops to drop a quarter in and asks, "Something wrong with the bell?"

Captain puts the bell to his ear, "rings" it and says as if puzzled, "I guess the batteries are dead."

"Do you mean the bell is run by...?" The mother realizes the Captain is kidding, laughs, wishes a merry Christmas and continues toward the shoe store.

A maintenance worker walks up to the kettle, drops a handful of coins into the red pot and remarks, "I can't hear anything from your bell."

Captain looks the man straight in the eye, opens and moves his mouth as if speaking, but emits no sounds. The worker laughs loudly and declares, "You're going to drive people with hearing aids crazy."

Two teenagers stop in their tracks, noticing the lack of ringing sounds.

"What are you doing with that bell?" one asks.

"I'm trying to win the NO-BELL peace prize."

The response, like that to many of the Captain's puns, is a groan followed by a laugh. They reach into their pockets to find money to donate.

Another donor deposits a dollar bill and asks, "Why no sound from the bell?"

Captain answers: "I forgot my sheet music and can't play it by ear."

Others give just a puzzled look. Captain answers them by claiming, "I bought this bell from a salesman who had laryngitis," or "This is a very religious bell, it has taken a vow of silence," or "Ever since I took this bell to see the Liberty Bell in Philadelphia, it has been speechless with awe."

Some Hispanic teenagers go by, remarking that the bell is not ringing. Captain replies: "No toca la campana en Ingles or en Espanol" ("The bell doesn't ring in English or in Spanish").

"My bell is upset because someone called him a 'dingaling'."

"I think my bell is sick. I called for a doctor from Indiana Bell, but they don't make mall-calls."

"Ever since my bell heard Big Ben, he has felt inadequate and not said a word."

To keep from repeating any jokes too often, the Captain keeps thinking them up between donors' visits and questions. He runs through some puns, trying to keep them from too obviously being groaners.

"He won't give a ring around the collar, either." "He's a school bell and doesn't ring on week-ends." "He's got a BELL-y ache." "He's just trying to get a BELL-y laugh."

Then the Captain decides to try out some longer lines:

"We had an argument and now he's not speaking to me." "When I finish paying for this bell, they're going to put the rest of it together for me." "This is a government bell and won't work overtime so near to the holidays." "I'm playing 'Carol of the Bells' but this bell forgot the words." "I'm playing a Hanukkah song, but this Gentile bell doesn't know the words." "This bell is very intelligent. It rings in English, Japanese and sign language." "The bell is on a rest break, but I'm not."

A teenage girl says, "I can't hear your bell." "That's good," the Captain answers. "It's an ultrasonic bell that can only be heard by dogs." The giggle in response shows that the shopper knows she is being joked with.

"My bell lost its voice." "Don't tell anyone, but my bell is not all there." "This bell is very shy." So the one-liners continue, opening up opportunities for the Captain to talk about his ministry and the significance of the Christmas message.

A nearby clerk who has been watching and listening comes over to the kettle, obviously wanting to talk. "You're doing very well without the bell. I've seen more smiles in the last couple of hours than all of yesterday before you came."

Each time a donation is made the Captain says to the giver: "Thank you very much. Have a holiday full of God's blessings."

The smiles, the opportunities for person-to-person contact, and the joy of making the best of a shopping mall's restrictions are added compensation for the work of a witty "kettle attendant."

MAJOR AND MRS. ARTHUR J. BROWN never failed to present a nativity play at each corps where they were stationed, and prided themselves on making each one even better than that of the year before.

In their tenth year of officership, when in command of the Army's ministry in Histon, Cambridgeshire, England, they realized that the previous ten performances had taken heavy toll on their angel dresses. It was high time, resolved Mrs. Major Audrey Brown, to renew their angelic wardrobe. How could this be done when funds were so limited? She hit on a great idea.

Though it would mean a lot of hard work for this year, since ambitiously they planned to employ a spectacular host of twenty-four angels, she asked each little girl to bring her an old white bed sheet, and she would work night and day making the angel dresses.

The nativity play was unsurpassed. Everyone said so. The sight of twenty-four little girls in sparkling white raiment, angelically innocent under the spotlights, melted the hardest heart. And, like the rich man in the parable, the Browns now had "much goods laid up for many years." They could eat, drink and be merry.

That was, until the first little innocent angel came and asked Mrs. Brown so sweetly if she could keep her angel dress as a nightie, for the undeniable reason that she had, after all, provided the sheet from which it was made.

The idea swept through the entire angel throng. Twenty-four little girls went home clutching the reward of their labors—twenty-four angel nightdresses.

The Browns re-stocked at their next corps appointment the following year, but were more prudent about where they went seeking for their old white sheets.

~

MRS. COMMISSIONER LOU KAISER, a gracious lady who provided a thoughtful ministry together with her husband, the late Commissioner Paul Kaiser, recounts the following Yuletide incidents:

A CHRISTMAS KETTLE stood in front of the lovely B. Altman store on Fifth Avenue, New York City. When a mother emerged with her two little girls from the store, she gave each child a dollar bill to drop into the kettle. Skipping back to her mother, one daughter exclaimed excitedly, "She spoke to me—she spoke to me." Her mother asked, "What did she say, darling?"

"She said, 'God bless you!' and I didn't even sneeze."

~

A RETIRED OFFICER who lived in Mt. Vernon, New York, volunteered all his time to the corps in that area. During the Christmas season, he manned one of the kettles on Main Street. He detected that when playing his concertina and singing the song, "Tell me the old, old story," the response from passersby increased significantly. Not surprisingly, it became his favorite, too.

One Saturday afternoon while he was singing the song, a group of teenage boys passed by. Sometime later in the day, the boys returned. It just so happened that the officer was again singing, "Tell me the old, old story."

"'I wonder why someone doesn't tell that old man the old, old story he wants to hear," remarked one sympathetic lad.

The "old man" was Brigadier Paul Kaiser, my father-in-law, father of Commissioner Paul S. Kaiser.

~

EVEN WHEN NOT MANNING A CHRISTMAS KETTLE, or holding a collecting box of any kind, uniformed Salvationists may sometimes find good-hearted members of the public asking them to pass on a donation because they were without change when they wanted to donate. Commissioner David A. Baxendale likes to recount the occasion when the stately mother of Commissioner Norman S. Marshall chose to shop after attending a Salvation Army annual New York Association dinner at the Waldorf Astoria early in December when Christmas kettles were to be seen on every street corner. She stopped at Macy's, then reputed to be the world's largest department store, but only long enough to buy a frying pan in the bargain basement.

But she couldn't hurry away. There were several other customers ahead of her. Her wait was not without reward, however. The sight of a Salvation Army lady holding a frying pan to hand to the clerk behind the counter struck a responsive chord in the hearts of three New Yorkers. All three dropped coins in her frying pan as they left.

~

IT SEEMS AFTER A LIFETIME of Salvation Army service officers still want to demonstrate their prowess in various fields when they join the ranks of the retired, including that of fund-raising. Either that or, because they know how burdensome financing can be, fellow sympathy compels them to give their active colleagues a helping hand.

As previously mentioned, Commissioner Denis Hunter became one of three ministers serving as chaplain at London's Gatwick Airport when he retired from active officership. But busy as he might be, when his corps officer made known the need for collectors, the good Denis humbly offered his services. Now in his seventies, but with a life time of finance schemes behind him, how could he withhold his expertise!

Assigned to stand outside an ASDA super store, he positioned himself strategically at a point where the outgoing shoppers from all twenty-four cash points had to pass him. Only an officer with his experience could have analyzed the situation so expertly. The excellence of this position must also have been noted by the public relations official of the Royal Society for the Protection of Cruelty to Animals (RSPCA). He had placed a life-size china Labrador dog at the same point, its plaintive eyes, shaggy tail, floppy ears—and box underneath its neck—making a haunting permanent appeal.

As a man, wife and six-year-old daughter approached him, the Commissioner's well-known smile intensified. "Mummy, give me something for the box, please," cried small daughter.

Without delay, mummy obliged and—as though playing the part of a wise man in a nativity play—small daughter advanced with her gift. BUT STRAIGHT INTO THE LABRADOR'S BOX WENT THE COINS.

"Hey," shouted father, "we thought you wanted the money for the Salvation Army man." The child dissolved into tears at this unexpected rebuke from dad. But the problem was soon resolved. More coins emerged and this time were put into the Salvation Army box by the tear-stained but now smiling little girl.

Driving away from the car park, the father circled back over to the Commissioner. He leaned confidentially out of the lowered window as he slowed down. "YOU'LL HAVE TO LET YOUR EARS GROW LONGER, WON'T YOU, MATE?!" he quipped with a grin.

～

IN LIMA, OHIO, WHEN CAPTAIN HOWARD W. BURR was the commanding officer, it was the custom for five service clubs to stand kettles for The Salvation Army for one whole day. It was a time of high spirits, enthusiasm and much competition. The manager of a local dime store played his part by providing a constant supply of hot coffee for the volunteer collectors.

All kinds of bizarre ideas were used to help raise money for the Army's Christmas program. One club member used a seeing-eye dog, wore dark glasses and held a tin cup, begging for funds. Others used a variety of containers, such as pots and antique pans. Little wonder then that one passer-by dropped his coins into one collector's cup of coffee. After all, for him there was little difference between putting it in the coffers and putting it in the coffee.

—*Howard Burr, Brigadier (R)*

～

FUNDING HIS FAST-GROWING SALVATION ARMY burdened the mind and heart of the Army's Founder, William Booth, almost from its birth in 1865. And Booth, strong in independence, hated asking for money, though he did so all his days. "It is not wise for a money-grabbing operation to be gone through whenever I appear," he growled at his son and Chief of Staff, Bramwell Booth, on whom he sought to rest the responsibility. "General Booth ought to be seen elsewhere than at Madam Tussaud's not asking for money," he added whimsically.

The cash flow problem was mostly borne by Bramwell. To his wife Florence he often explained his anxiety: "Darling, I am very burdened about money. I don't know where to turn. Surely the Lord will help us." Their eldest child,

Catherine, aged four, and Mary, aged two, early learned to finish evening prayers: 'Dear Lord, send the Army a lot of money to make Papa happy'." (*The General Next to God* by Richard Collier.)

The concern was shared by his officers. One officer, though existing on most meager support himself, wrote his General: "By going without pudding every day for a year, I calculate I can save fifty shillings. This I will do, and will remit the amount named as quickly as possible."

Deeply touched by such devotion, Booth declared none must go without pudding for a year. But all Salvationists could be asked to go without for one week. Thus "Self-Denial" week was born to touch both hearts and pockets of his followers. Then it was expanded to a public appeal, with a nationwide distribution of appeal envelopes in Great Britain. Not until 1980 was there the first of several name-changes, but the foot-slogging method of envelope distribution and collection remained.

Inevitably, such annual appeals involve the hundreds of collectors in all kinds of escapades, from being chased by defending dogs to total misunderstandings—as happened when Major Arthur J. Brown (producer of angelic nativity plays) was an agent for the then Salvation Army Assurance Society in Scotland, prior to becoming an officer.

A cadet had been sent from the London Training College to assist with the annual Self-Denial appeal and to gain useful experience for his future officership. He was assigned to an officer who decided to reduce the workload by not using the appeal envelopes, but taking a collecting box and making just one call at a house.

Knocking at one door, he was asked by the lady who answered, "Is this a new way of collecting?"

"Yes," answered the cadet. "It is much quicker and easier, and I am rather pressed for time."

To his delight, the lady dropped two half-crowns in his box. As he bounded down the steps, she called after him: "You can mark my Assurance Society book next week."

IN CANADA, THE FOOT-SLOGGING ASPECT OF THE SELF-DENIAL APPEAL GAVE WAY in 1942 to a more highly structured RED SHIELD APPEAL. The Army seized the opportunity to capitalize on the immense affection gained through the wartime Red Shield Clubs and mobile canteens serving the forces both at home and overseas. The appeal envelope was abandoned. Both Salvationist and non-Salvationist volunteers were recruited to call on households and provide receipts for donations given.

Lt.-Colonel Bob Chapman recalls Red Shield collecting as a young officer in a rural community primarily composed of German-speaking people. When he knocked on one door, the lady who responded commented, "Oh, another new man." Bob made no reply but simply followed her as she led him to the basement and left him standing there alone.

Suddenly, he realized that she had mistakenly presumed, on seeing his uniform, he was there to read the gas or electricity meter. He wondered what to do. Feeling rather embarrassed, he waited a moment or two then took his leave, wishing her a good day.

He has often wondered since what the good lady thought when the real meter reader arrived.

THE NOTED U.S. ACTRESS, TALLULAH BANKHEAD (1903-68), famous for her flamboyant lifestyle, is said to have dropped a fifty dollar bill into the tambourine held out to her by a Salvation Army collector.

Waving aside the Salvationist's thanks, Tallulah said, "Don't bother to thank me. I know what a perfectly ghastly season it's been for you Spanish dancers." (Reported in *The Faber Book of Anecdotes*.)

Eccentrics aren't confined to the wealthy classes, but it was another very rich lady who left a lasting impression on teenager Fred Norton, of St. Albans, England, at Christmas time. A demanding caroling program traditionally took the band to every part of the city and surrounding districts. It meant non-stop hard work for the bandsmen.

In a very well-to-do part of the town stood a particularly large and grand house. The occupant was known to be a very wealthy spinster. But the mansion was set in grounds of its own, a distance from the road. So Fred's father, who was bandmaster for thirty-six years, decided that only a quartet should go to the lady, while the remainder of the band continued to cover the district. The four, Fred among them, trekked their way up the lengthy, tree-lined drive and commenced to play seasonal music.

The door was soon opened by a man servant in red and gold livery, black knee breeches and black buckled shoes. In tones like that of a town crier he announced, "Miss S......" presents her compliments and requests you to play the hymn-tune 'Helmsley' ."

The quartet was only too happy to oblige. Their rendition was rewarded with a substantial donation and the four returned to the main party thoroughly elated.

The following year the incident was remembered and the same quartet advanced on the mansion with eager anticipation. The frosty air resounded again with "Helmsley." Scarcely had they played the first few bars than the door was flung open and the same servant, attired as before, stood there.

"MISS S........SAYS WILL YOU PLEASE STOP PLAYING THAT UNSUITABLE TUNE AND GO AWAY."

Thoroughly chastened and deflated, the four slunk away, pondering on the eccentricity of the wealthy.

IF FOR SALVATION ARMY MUSICIANS Christmas is hard work, for Army officers the season to be jolly can be utterly exhausting. Who better to tell of the physical, mental and even spiritual demands made on them than Colonel Rowland D. Hughes, master of the pen dipped in iridescent ink!

BY DECEMBER 26, SALVATION ARMY CORPS officers—bushed, baggy- eyed and bedeviled by full many an ache and pain—could do with much prayer and much sympathy. They're physically drained. If the Lord, or their leaders, could or would grant them their wish, they'd probably plump for a fun-filled week in the intensive care unit of the nearest hospital. And who can blame them? They're fed up to here with the annual effort.

They've stood for so many hours on so many drafty corners in rain, hail, snow and gloom of night that they're bugged by bronchitis, laryngitis, pharyngitis, sinusitis and every other "itis" between lips and lungs known to top-level smarties in the medical racket.

They've played "I Heard the Bells," "Carol of the Bells," and "Jingle Bells" so often that even now (two days after they have dragged in the pots for the last time) their heads are still ringing, a post-Christmas complaint known as "bells in the belfry syndrome."

They've listened to so many grim stories of need from those suffering pain, injustice and stark tragedy (while we, on another wavelength altogether, have been thrilling to the angelic tidings of universal joy, peace and goodwill), that on several occasions their faith has been sorely tried when disquieting evidence has suggested that the Bethlehem chorus seems harshly out of tune with the awful realities in the world of today.

They've put 3,426 miles on the corps station wagon since Thanksgiving. Picked up potato salad from the Elks. Franks and beans from the Masons. Bread, cake and rolls from the Shop and Save. Canned goods from grade schools. Toys, games and clothing from generous merchants.

They've painted kettles, set up kettles, relieved other weary kettle workers and, with unvarying cheerfulness, thanked donors with a hearty "Merry Christmas!" or "God bless you!" even though they were so cold they felt sure rigor mortis had already set in. Ad libbed full many an account of the Army's Yule ministry at service clubs and church circles. And counted and wrapped pennies, nickels, dimes and quarters until spirits flagged and flesh failed.

They've decorated the auditorium. Arranged holiday parties for the Cradle Roll, Sunbeams, Guards, the Home League, the Sunday school and other corps and community groups. Dispatched scores or hundreds of food orders together with greetings apropos of the season. Been at the beck and call of the mayor, the police department, the fire department, the family planning council, the fathers for the improvement of teenagers, the mothers for the improvement of fathers, the sons of liberty unlimited, the daughters of the new breed and the golf-widows' guild. Filled in whenever and wherever there was a breakdown. And, with an eye cocked on last year's income figures, worried the livelong day about weather, workers and weariness.

And that's not all. Those are only their "moonlighting" activities. Concurrently, they've had to keep their normal corps program up to snuff.

Thus they've visited the sick. Married the young. Buried the dead. Taught a Sunday school class. Met regularly with the senior citizens. Preached twice on Sundays. Rushed coffee and crullers to crashes, cave-ins and conflagrations. Kept the Army's "new and improved" financial records up-to-date. Mailed weekly reports to D.H.Q. Attended divisional functions. Counseled mixed-up couples. Waxed and buffed floors when the janitor took off for parts unknown. Poured oil on troubled waters when a couple of kooky comrades (bristling because they weren't top dogs in the kingdom) caused a bit of unpleasantness.

They've sat in with city bigwigs to discuss welfare problems. Presented the Army's position on pot, permissiveness, promiscuity and pornography before the monthly meeting of the ministerial association. And, on more than one occasion, seen their schedules get hopelessly snarled via untoward incidents and unforeseen developments.

Now, after six or seven weeks of this "mission impossible," they're at home in a state of near collapse. They want to forget the whole holly-jolly bit. They're glad it's over. They're grateful they survived. So grateful that, at day's end, while they hoarsely whisper their "Now I lay me down to sleep" from beneath the sheets, they'll devoutly thank the Lord for His loving kindness in pulling them through the effort and for seeing to it that they won't have to go through another Christmas for a whole year.

And that's unspeakably sad, unutterably tragic. For no one should be so busy or bleary-eyed that, by and large, they miss the soft rustle of angels' wings, the breath-taking sight of the star, the music of the spheres, or—more's the pity—the Christ Child himself.

Perhaps to an extent wholly unrealized by most of us, corps officers miss much of this. Frenetically engaged in an all-out effort to "keep the pot boiling," in an effort to bring cheer and comfort to the dark streets of the community, to the sadly born, the poorly circumstanced and the unfortunately environed; in an on-the-phone, in-and-out-of-the-car, up-and-down-stairs activity that carries into nights and weekends, they scarcely have any time to join the shepherds in the rude stable and to kneel in awe and wonder before the crib of the newborn king.

For our money, they're tops. They're the greatest. They are an inspiring example of Christian leadership, of Salvationism at its best. We're proud of them and deem it a distinct honor to pay tribute to them.

May God bless them in overflowing measure and encourage their hearts by the blessed assurance that in that Happy Land, wherein are many mansions, there will be no poor, no needy, no distressed, no disadvantaged and—NO KETTLES AND NO CHRISTMAS EFFORTS.

CHAPTER 16

MY FRIEND CHARLIE

IT WILL CAUSE NO SURPRISE TO ANY STUDENT of human nature that Salvation Army officers thoroughly enjoy "pulling the leg" of those holding senior rank. The "great and the good," those who move in the top flights of administration and tell the lower orders what is good for them, can expect at times to be the butt of some joking.

The opportunities for such good-natured leg-pulling are few and far between, but they are seized upon eagerly when they do occur. The UK Territory's annual three-day councils, usually held at the Hayes Conference Centre in Swanwick, Derbyshire, provide opportunity at the end of each day for informal get together by officers. Between some hearty impromptu communal singing, tales are told and recollections revived.

MAJOR ARTHUR J. BROWN'S rhyming skills have often been in demand at such times and wisely he would usually "just happen to have a verse or two in my pocket." Many would judge he was at his wittiest when he wrote, "My Friend Charlie."

My Friend Charlie

Folks often ask why I've never aspired
To be General, or assistant at least.
Well, it happened one day, in a strange sort of way,
That my hopes of promotion all ceased.

'Twas our very first married appointment,
The smallest the Army could boast;
The division itself was not all that big,
About sixteen square miles at the most.

But our divis'nal commander was happy,
For it helped him in his sort of way,
And over his desk hung his motto:
"You must get it done by today."

He couldn't stand letters or writing
Or forms or returns or that lot;
He insisted we TOOK our returns in to him
To settle things there on the spot.

"I'll be having your band in October"
Though he'd never asked me, for we'd none;
Or "Add up those columns of figures,
And see that the totals are done."

The Majors rode in in their Daimlers,
The Captains went in on the bus;
But it wasn't that easy for others -
Well, not for Lieutenants like us.

We were miles away from the office,
And I'd cycle there in the rain,
Stuff my "budget" into my coat pocket
And peddle back homewards again.

I'd ne'er see a soul to converse with,
They were filling in forms or at tea,
And so fully absorbed in their business
They never gave any to me.

But I must tell you now about Charlie—
I ought to have told you before—
A chimp who'd been part educated
By the man who was living next door.

Now Charlie was bright as a button,
The sort that you really could like;
He could juggle and balance and count up to six
And ride on a two-wheeler bike.

He sure loved his bike did our Charlie,
He rode it all over the park;
He'd a bell he would ring before knocking you down
And lights to light up after dark.

Well, one Thursday morning in summer,
When I'd just got my books to make sense,
I was ready to go to the office
When I chanced to look over the fence.

Poor Charlie was sitting dejected,
I'd ne'er seen the chimp look so grim.
I inquired from his owner what ailed him
And asked, 'What's the matter with him?'

"It's his bike," says our neighbor, "it's been stolen,
Outside the chip shop, if you please.
He wants me to buy him another,
So he's sulking now there, as you sees."

And there on the spot I'd a brainwave,
It came like a bolt from the blue;
So brilliant I scarcely could credit;
I knew now just what I should do.

I beckoned to Charlie: "Come on, lad,"
He tried on my cap for a start;
With my uniform trousers and tunic
You just couldn't tell us apart.

I gave him my bike and a satchel,
And careful directions as well;
He sped down the road like a rocket,
With hand signals, ringing his bell.

Well, of course, I was just a bit anxious,
A little uneasy, in case
They rumbled my scheme at headquarters
Of Charlie being sent in my place.

But there really was no need to worry,
For half-an-hour later, no more,
He sailed down the road with my budget
And brought it safe right to my door.

So that was the pattern thereafter;
Each Thursday in sunshine or rain,
He'd take my returns to the office
And bring back the budget again.

But one beautiful day in September,
I ne'er dreamed as he walked out the door
That I'd never again see my old faithful friend,
Or my bike—come to that—any more.

For the Brigadier down at "The Castle"
Was what they call "sick of the corps,"
And he'd just told the Colonel that morning
He was not stopping there any more.

The Colonel was almost demented,
And couldn't think what he might do;
As I said, he liked "instant decisions,"
But now "instant options" were few.

For being the end of September,
The whole of the officer race
Was off on vacation to Butlins*,
So he'd no one to put in his place.

Well, no one, that is, except Charlie,
Who swept through the door in a whiz;
He seized Charlie's hand with emotion
And told him "The Castle" was his.

Since that day I've never seen Charlie,
Though he tackled the job with some zest.
*He's Commissioner now on some tropical isle
And I'm stuck down here in South West.*

*Butlins is a holiday camp. A chain of them founded by
Canadian Billy Butlin operates in Britain. The Army takes over
one camp each year for holidays, fellowship and worship. Some
4,000 attend.*

CHAPTER 17

THEY SAID SO

"JOY SHALL BE IN HEAVEN over one sinner that repenteth, more than over ninety and nine just persons, which need no repentance."

—Jesus Christ (Luke 15:7)

"These things have I spoken unto you, that my joy might remain in you, and that your joy might be full."

—Jesus Christ (John 15:11)

"Our cheerful banners are unfurled,
For Christ has overcome the world."
    —Catherine Baird (Salvation Army Song Book No. 5)

"There's not much fun in physic, but there's a good deal of physic in fun."

—C. W. George (quoted in Keep Smiling)

"Humor promotes mental health and instills creativity. It motivates us. And motivated, we perform better at our jobs. When fun is part of the workplace, the organization is happier and stronger; teamwork prevails. When the job becomes fun, life becomes a lot easier too."

—*Gerris Dakers (Canadian Health Care Guild, Edmonton, Canada).*

"He traveled with all his worldly goods in a small Gladstone bag and often skipped his meals, sometimes because he was too busy to eat and sometimes because he was too poor. He was lonely—he was always lonely—but not unhappy. Indeed, few men have lived lives more serene than he. He prayed long, but not too long, read his Bible, but also the newspapers, and always retained his sense of humor."

—*Bernard Watson (in* Soldier Saint, *biography of George Scott Railton, William Booth's first Lieutenant Hodder and Stoughton Ltd.).*

"The life of a soul-saver is the grandest, merriest, strangest life that can be lived on earth - the life of Jesus over again in us. It will cost you all, but it will be a good bargain at that."

—*George Scott Railton (in autograph album of Saunders family, Halifax, Nova Scotia, with whom he stayed for ten days after missing the boat to London through being too engrossed in conducting an open-air meeting—the first Salvation Army street meeting to be held in Canada).*

Thank God for laughter!
How dull the day that passes without a smile;
How long the hours without a spark of humor!
How subtle of God to create beings who could laugh at

themselves even when things go wrong!
And if we are made in the image of God,
Is he a laughing God?
When God is not weeping, does he laugh at the antics of
      man?
      —*Frank Topping* (Lord of Time —*Lutterworth Press*).

Joy is the wine that God is ever pouring
Into the hearts of those who strive with him,
Light'ning their eyes to vision and adoring,
Strength'ning their arms to warfare glad and grim.
      —G. A. Studdert Kennedy (*The Unutterable Beauty*—
Mowbray).

"The first symptom of the emotionally ill person is his
lack of laughter."
      —*Dr. John McBride, Phoenix, Ariz., psychotherapist.*

"Never trust a theologian who doesn't have a sense of
humor...Anyone who reads the synoptic gospels with a rela-
tive freedom from suppositions might be expected to see that
Christ laughed, and that He expected others to laugh, but our
capacity to miss this aspect of His life is phenomenal. We are
so sure He was always deadly serious that we often twist His
words in order to make them conform to our preconceived
mold. A misguided piety has made us fear that acceptance of
His obvious wit and humor would somehow be mildly blas-
phemous or sacrilegious...The critics of Christ have, on the
whole, been as blind to His humor as have His admirers...If
Christ laughed a great deal, as the evidence shows, and if He
is what He claimed to be, we cannot avoid the logical conclusion that there is laughter and gaiety in the heart of God."
—*Elton Trueblood* (*quoted in* The Joyful Christ *by Cal Samra,
published by Harper and Row*).

"The most balanced people I know possess a certain quality of joy, have a keen sense of humor, and laugh with the easy spontaneity of a small child. The unbalanced rarely show joy or flashes of humor. Humor is a balancing, disarming and therefore peacemaking force that touches on the divine."
—*Cal Samra,* The Joyful Christ.

"A cheerful heart is good medicine; but a crushed spirit dries up the bones."
—*Proverbs 17:22 NIV.*

"Against the assault of humor, nothing can stand."
—*Mark Twain.*

"We ought to present ourselves to God as we are. The relationship ought to be with God as it is with your closest friend. If you feel like joking with God, joke with Him."
—*Jesuit Father Arthur McGovern, University of Detroit.*

"When it comes to religion, anything that attempts to be even mildly humorous threatens closed minds. I've never figured out why. I grant that some attempts at humor are tasteless...but I'm not talking about attacks on the truly sacred. The veil of the sacred seems to cover anything associated with religion, and that veil shelters all manner of pomposities, absurdities and just plain baloney—all of which are legitimate targets for humor."
—*Joel Wells, Catholic satirist.*

"Then Abraham fell upon his face, and laughed..."— *Genesis 17:17*. "And the Lord said unto Abraham, 'Wherefore did Sarah laugh...?' Then Sarah denied, saying 'I laughed not;' for she was afraid. And he said, 'Nay, but thou didst laugh'."

—*Genesis 18:13,15.*

"The Lord laughs at the wicked, for he knows their day is coming."

—*Psalm 37:13 NIV.*

A little group of councilors were discussing Denry. "What a card," said one, laughing joyously. "He's a rare 'un, no mistake." "Of course, this'll make him more popular than ever," said another. "We've never had a man to touch him for that."

"And yet," demanded Councilor Barlow, "what's he done? Has he ever done a day's work in his life? What great cause is he identified with?"

"He's identified," said the speaker, "with the great cause of cheering us all up."

—*Arnold Bennett* (The Card).